Play & Learn Squash

N. Jain

KHEL SAHITYA KENDRA
7/26, Ansari Road, Daryaganj,
New Delhi-110002

Published by:
KHEL SAHITYA KENDRA
7/26, Ansari Road, Darya Ganj, New Delhi-110002
Ph.: (O) 011-43551324, 42564726, 47090343
(M) 9811088729, (Fax) 011-42564726
(Res.) 47091605
E-mail: khelsahitya1@rediffmail.com
Website: www.khelsahitya.com, www.kskpublisher.com

ISBN 978-81-7524-126-8

PRINTED IN INDIA 2026

Printed by:
ASIAN OFFSET PRINTERS
Delhi

Laser Typesetting by:
K.S.K. DTP UNIT, DELHI

CONTENTS

1

INTRODUCTION

Kipling wrote that "Allah created the English mad-the maddest of all mankind !" But the Irish, Scottish, and Welsh are affected by the same malady {the relatively sober scots, remember, gave us golf, an incredibly complicated ritual for deciding who shall pay for the drinks}. The British as a whole have always had a national genius- and genius, it is said, is akin to madness- for inventing games, and a national compulsion for playing them. So they acquired an unparalleled network of games for all tastes and all weathers. And every game was exported by the services and by emigrants during the expansion of the British Empire. Now the Empire has gone: but Britain's infectious madness for playing games finds an enthusiastic response from every nation in the world. The British may still be "the maddest of all mankind ". But there are some pretty close runners-up, not least the descendants of British settlers in Australia, New Zealand, and South Africa.

Yet the national compulsion for playing game soon struck a sang, since games were traditionally played outdoors- and Britain has a climate that the cynical describe as "eight months of winter and four months of bad weather". This was a challenge to the national genius for invention, and the British came up with a peculiar assortment of indoor games. Squash was the best of them. During those decades, the manufacturers' figures for the sales of British sports equipment showed clearly enough which way the trend was heading: in terms of percentage increases, squash had advanced more than twice as fast as any other sport, indoor or outdoor. In that decade, the sales figures for squash gear had more than doubled. Nor was the boom limited to the rank and file. For the decade ended with a historic triumph, at the very summit of the game, by a Cornishman called Jonah Barrington, who became the first British player in the history of the game to win the open and amateur championships in the same season. The nation of its birth was once more leading the way as squash roared ahead in the popularity polls throughout the world. All of which bring us to the question.

What are We Playing at?

First of all, squash is played in a pit 32 ft. long and 21 ft. wide. The front wall is 15 ft. high, the back wall 7 ft. high, so that the side walls are 8 ft. higher at the front of the court than they are at the back. The upper limits of the side walls sink gradually from front to back, like a descending line on a graph. So that you can get in and out of the court without using a ladder, a door fits flush into the back wall.

Basically the game is a little like lawn tennis- except that both players are on the same side of the " net", which in this case is a strip of metal, known as the " tin", at the bottom of the front wall. The players have a racket each

and take it in turns to hit a small, soft black ball above the tin. The ball must go over the tin before touching the floor. Then the other player can volley it, or allow it to bounce once. He loses the rally if he allow the ball to bounce more than once- or hits it into the tin; or onto the walls on or above the lines marking the upper limits of the court. Or onto the lights or any other fittings in the roof. A point can be recorded only by the player who is serving. When he loses a rally, he loses the right to serve {the excellence of this system is that the player who is serving can be as adventurous as he likes in choosing his shots, because a mistake will not cost him a point}. The basic idea is that the first player to score nine points wins a game, and the first player to win three games wins the match.. But if a game reaches 8-all, the player who is not serving can decide whether the game will go to the first man to win another point, or to the first man to win two more points. So the farthest any game can go is 10-9.

A game is started by a player standing with at least one foot in a service box and not touching any of the lines around it. At the beginning of a match the right to serve is decided by spinning a racket. The server may start from either box, but after winning each point he must change over to the other box. The server throws the ball up and hits it direct onto the front wall. The ball must hit the front wall above a line { called the "cut line"} marked across it, and then rebound over the "shortline" { painted across the floor} into the opponent' half court- though the opponent may, if he chooses, return the ball before it bounces. After hitting the front wall, the service may touch any other wall before it bounces into the opponent's half-court. The receiver must return the ball before it has bounced twice, so that it hits the front wall anywhere above the tin. But the service is the only stroke that has to be hit direct onto the front wall. Any other stroke in a rally can be cannoned off another wall, so long as it eventually hits the front well above the tin before bouncing. Apart from the service, it doer not matter where the ball bounces. So a rally goes on until one player puts the ball into the tin or out of court, or allows it to bounce twice.

There are four basic shots- the drive, the drop} shot, the lob, and the angle { with its brother, the boast}. The first three are similar to the same strokes in lawn tennis. But the angle and boast are strokes played on to a side wall so that the ball rebounds onto the front wall. The ball may even be cannoned off or three other walls before it hits the front wall. But once the ball leaves the racket, it must not bounce until it has struck the front wall. It is the variety of side-wall shots { plus the fact that squash is the only popular game in which both players are on the same side of the " net"} that gives squash its special appeal. The presence of the walls also means that even novices can put every service into court without difficulty, and can then keep the rallies going for a ling time.

All this may seem a rather strange basis for the fastest growing sport of our time. But give it a try: and the boom will soon explain itself. Squash can be played by either sex, at any age, at any time, in any weather. It asks no favours of the climate. It ignores rain and darkness outside. For boys and girls, men and women, whether 16 or 60, it offers concentrated competitive exercise- and exercise that is as absorbing for the mind as it is healthy for the body . Its nature can be adjusted to the needs of the individual: its pace gentle or fierce, its texture delicate or strong. At its highest level all these qualities mingle, even in the course of one rally-the quick and the slow, the violent and the cunning. The only perquisite for an exciting and satisfying match is that the two players concerned should have a similar ability. Even if this condition is not met, pleasant exercise is still available, as long as the better player directs his shots to areas where they will not be too difficult for his opponent to retrieve.

For the novice, the game's rewards are immediate, since squash permits rapid progress- up to a point- for anyone with even a modest ball sense. After only a few hours on court, two beginners will know enough to have a vigorous and enjoyable match. Later the game's mask of simplicity falls away. But a glittering treasure house stands revealed; a treasure house in which the lightning of sudden shafts of speed flickers around the caressing brushwork of deception. Where all seemed straight forward, the novice, in wonderment, finds himself in a furiously complicated world where geometry becomes a game, where animal energy is married to the mental agility of the chessboard. He is playing " physical chess"- fighting a battle of wits, at high speed. In short, squash can be as simple, or as complex, as you care to make it.

Squash is perfectly in tune with the tempo of the modern age. It only asks an hour of our time, the hour including the whole process of changing, playing taking a shower, and changing back again. In that hour anyone can take exactly as much exercise as he or she wants- no more, and no less. No time is wasted by trotting off to fetch the ball when it has been hit out of court- the walls do the fetching for us. The game is cheap to play, and in terms of fitness alone offers a dazzling investment all the year round. But the young may prefer it as a complement to some outdoor game, and in this respect, too Squash is superb. It tones up the whole system, sharpens reflexes, improves coordination of hand and eye, and does not neglect a muscle. If there is a cricketer of a lawn tennis player, a footballer or a rugby player, who says Squash is no use to him, then he has never played the game.

Like a good party, Squash is congenial and noisy { when two good players are in action, a court can sound like a pistol range}. Whether we play in some remote corner of the provinces, or in the spacious comforts of the west End social clubs, Squash provides championship of a quality that few sports can equal and none can surpass. Whatever we may ask of a game, Squash has all the answers: and those answers make us a little healthier, a little more alert, a little more considerate, a little better equipped for our every day lives. We can expect no more from any sport.

How it happened

In the days before shops, when our ancestors had either to grow their food or catch it, there was no need to invent game. The tricky business of staying alive was enough to keep them on their toes. But as the need for these primitive pursuits reached, sport began to develop, notably the elementary exercise of running. Later came ball games, in all their ramifications. We started knocking the ball at each other, or against a wall { "fives", denoting the fingers of one hand, is still with us}. Then, as the richly diverse texture of sport became woven into the pattern of history, an odd assortment of rackets came into use. In the 19th century the famous public school at harrow, just outside century the famous public school at Harrow, just outside London, was already a thriving centre for the old game of rackets {still played, on a small scale}. From this emerged the germ of the game we now call squash rackets, which outgrew its parent long ago. So the place of birth was Harrow. The date of birth? There can be no specific answer. All that can safely be said be said is that Squash evolved as an informal variant of rackets {one of the walls used was the outside of the rackets court}, about the middle of the 19th century. There were a series of makeshift courts, accidental rather than deliberate in their structure. In the late 1860s, and the 1870s, the first vague, tentative steps were made towards a standard court. The word "Squash" was also becoming accepted. Unlike its parent game of rackets, the variant was played with a soft, hollow ball { sometimes with holes in it} that "Squashed" and made appropriate noises when it hit the walls. In 1883 the first court designed specifically for Squash was built by a Harrow man, at Oxford. By 1886 Squash was beginning to achieve some sort of recognition as an independent game. In succeeding decades, courts were built in private dwellings and in the London social clubs{ still the game's spiritual home}. Squash was growing up.

The Tennis and Rackets Association { formed in 1907 }- and we should point out that tennis was the "royal " or "real" game played indoors, as distinct from lawn tennis- appointed a subcommittee to draw up some rules for squash and administer the game. In 1911 the Association laid down standard measurements for squash courts, but these did not take their final shape until after the 1914-18 war. Early in the twenties came the first national championship for men and women, though the United States {1906}, South Africa {1910}, and Canada {1911} had got off the mark a lot sooner. The squash rackets Association had an inaugural meeting in 1928, became officially established a year later, and took over the administration of the game from the Tennis and Rackets Association {the three sports remain inseparably linked by the

common denominator of indoor courts, though squash quickly outstripped the other two in popularity. Associations had been formed in the United States and Canada but in spite of the fact that they used the word "squash", our friends across the Atlantic played with a hard ball on a slightly different type of court, so that their game developed on vastly contrasting lines from its English counterpart. In retrospect, this was a lamentable digression, since it meant that the Americans and Canadians had backed the wrong horse. They developed a game that fell midway between squash and rackets and therefore left them out on a limb-playing a game that had taken root nowhere else. Nowadays the American and Canadian game has no more in common with British squash than British squash has with rackets, or rugby union with rugby league. But one overseas nation backed the right horse, because in 1910 South Africa formed an association who promoted the British game as distinct from the American.

With the S.R.A. fully in control of an expanding young game, the 1930s were boom years. The manufacture of a slower ball made the technique of squash both more subtle and more spectacular. It became far more skilful and strenuous than its counterpart across the Atlantic. The whole technical and tactical scope of the game was adjusted and expanded, and this inevitably marked the last break with rackets, which had giver squash its first players and its first administrators. The women's S.R.A. was formed in 1934. Squash clubs sprang up everywhere. More overseas countries began to take up the game. The seeds took root in Australia, though in those days no one could have guessed that, a quarter of a century later, Australia would lead the world in a starting exploitation of the commercial possibilities of vast blocks of public courts, where anyone could play at any time.

In squash, as in so many other spheres of human

endeavour, the 1939-45 war was an interregnum. Afterwards came a huge leap forward, with squash fast becoming a world game. The 1950s were great years. It was then that the boon really hit Australia. It was then that the wondrous family of Pathans, the Khans, lifted the game to a new plane. It was then that British schools began to shake off their traditional prejudice against individual as opposed to team games, so that squash became an increasingly respectable part of the sporting curriculum. The game pushed its rots through the entire community. Squash was no longer the almost exclusive prerogative of public schoolboys and west End social clubs. All this was exciting, because if the apex of the pyramid is to be high, than the base must be broad. But perhaps the chief reason for the game's breakneck advance, everywhere, was the many special qualities that made it perfectly adjusted to the bustling, quick-thinking tempo of modern life. Competition became fiercer, international rivalry more intense. Tours multiplied. Every season contingents of rugged, superbly trained players from overseas came to London for the big championships. With a few individual exceptions, the British game was not geared to competition of this fervour. From a playing point of view the parent nation of squash seemed to be in its dotage. The Australians and Egyptians came to the fore, contrasted in style but equally dedicated to success. From overseas came rumblings of discontent. Why should the world's best players always have to travel to London for the "world" championships? Why should Britain administer the game when they could no longer set the pace on court? The criticisms were soundly based. The young players of overseas nations- players not yet good enough to earn an expensive trip to London-needed and deserved the inspiration of watching the world's best players on their own courts. And so far as its administration was concerned, squash had clearly become too big a sport for one national association to handle,

Fortunately the S.R.A. had appointed in 1955, a secretary whose diplomacy and unparalleled knowledge of the game were to server them well when the crisis came. Mr. John Horry did not allow the discontent to grow. With foresight and initiative, he and his colleagues on the S.R.A. Drew together the scattered threads of the world game. Thus the post-war expansion led, in January, 1966, to an international conference in London. The delegates decided to from the International Squash Rackets Federation, to take over responsibility for the rules of the game, to coordinate tours, and to settle any international disputes. They also decided that the first official world team and individual championships would be played in Australia in August, 1967. The constitution drawn up at that conference was ratified during 1966 by the seven founder members-Australia, Great Britain, India, New Zealand, Pakistan, South Africa, and the United Arab Republic.

The Way Ahead

Squash has now become the victim of its own virtues. There are not enough courts for the people who want to play.

There is not enough room for the people who want to watch. In Britain, commercial speculators and local authorities probably hold the key to the future in the way providing new courts, since the prime need is for public as distinct from private courts. These would also raise the level of Britain's national team by broadening the basis of recruitment. A national ranking list, as in lawn tennis, would be another incentive for those players prepared to work at the game instead of merely playing at it. Standards could also be improved- and inevitably will be- by a longer and stronger competitive season, with inter-club and intercountry competitions achieving a higher status. The advent of an itinerant world championship may help indirectly, by reducing overseas participation in the two British championships to such an extent that it will no longer be necessary to sandwich them together, in December and January in both during one trip on London. But it may now be possible to strengthen the British season by holding one championship in the middle and the other towards the end.

2

HISTORY OF SQUASH

It is very difficult to mention the exact origin of Squash but because this game was developed from rackets it can be assumed that it should be first played in walled yards of London taverns and prisons in early 19th century. Inexplicably, in the 1820s, rackets travelled the few miles north-west to infinitely more sedate surroundings of Harrow school. Sometime in the next decade, almost certainly by accident, a softer ball than that used normally in rackets found its way on to the courts at Harrow. Thus two slightly different variations of the same theme known as harder and squash—depending on the ball used—began to develop.

In 1850 two roofless rackets courts were built at the school and when in 1864 a covered court was erected and four squash courts appeared on the site of one of the earlier roofless versions the two games took an entirely separate identities. Squash doubtless grew in popularity in the years that followed but, apart from building of first-ever privately owned court by former Harrow pupil Vernon Harcourt in Oxford in 1883, little or nothing of its progress is charted.

The first known published reference to the game is a mention in The Badminton Library of Sports and Pastimes in 1890: "There are now in existence in England several private houses with a more elaborate squash court attached, built indeed like a smaller hardball court". The first in-depth explanation of the game and its rules appeared in The Boys' Own Paper in 1893. Author Somerville Gilbey introduced the game with these words: "Squash, a corruption of squash racquets, is a familiar name of to all Harrow boys and might be so with advantage to other boys as well because it designates a capital game which, without requiring any large expenditure of pocket-money or amount of apparatus, can be played anywhere there are walls. Give a Harrow boy a wall—if a blank one so much the better— and two others, or even one other, at right angles to it, with a clear space between, and the probability is it wound not be long before he is busy at squash rackets".

It is interesting to note that Gilbey sometimes refereed to the game as "rugby squash" because he believed it had its origins in the rugby fives courts at Harrow. The first book on squash, entitled The Game of Squash, written by world champion rackets and tennis player Eustace Miles, was published in 1901. Miles wrote that even though there had not yet been an official championship, very few competitions and no professionals devoted solely to the game, thousands of people throughout the world played and enjoyed squash. Meanwhile the game was already establishing itself in America.

In 1891 the Philadelphia Racket Club had built a squash court and when, in 1907, the United State's Squash Racquets Association was formed and held the world's first national championship, the club provided the winner, John A. Miskey. A year later a USSRA national team championship was held. The Americans preferred the use of a harder ball and longer narrow courts and, because of lack of standardisation of courts and equipment, the American game rapidly developed its own identity. This rift has never been healed and today the Americans still play predominantly the hardball game while in the rest of the world the softball or international game is unchallenged.

In 1907 the Tennis and Rackets Association was formed in England with a special committee to look after the interests of squash. This was followed by the forming of two other national associations, one in South Africa in 1910 which decided to conform to the rules as being played in Britain and the other in 1911 in Canada. By 1920 Britain still had no squash association of its own but there was plenty of activity.

The first two match challenges for the professional championship of the British Isles took place between Charles Read and Oke Johnson and this was the forerunner of the two main British events—the Amateur and Open Championships. Over in America the hardball game was developing apace and the donation of a cup by Mr. Henry G. Lapham of Boston stimulated a match in 1922 between USA and Canada—an occurrence which makes the Lapham Cup the oldest international fixture.

By beating her sister Nancy Mrs. Joyce Cave became Britain's first-ever Amateur champion in February 1922 and it was not until the following year that the men's event was inaugurated and Tommy Jameson crowned champion. In 1923 the Tennis and Racket Association formalised standards for the court and ball. In the following year the playing rules were established and in 1925 the dimensions for the racket were laid down.

15-point game changed to 9-point game in Britain in year 1926 and as the Americans had already standardised their rules on play and equipment, this further cemented the rift between the American and British games. By the mid-twenties long flannel trousers were giving way to shorts, court walls were being plastered and team events were proving popular. England

and America were competing in international competition which posed problems for players attempting to adapt from one ball to another.

Charles Arnold, Britain's first squash professional, was quoted at the time: "the ball is a very vexed question in squash" some things never change. The Squash Rackets Association was founded on 13 December 1928 in the Royal Automobile Club in Pall Mall, London. Although affiliated to the Tennis and Rackets Association, it took over complete responsibility for the British game throughout the world. Its first executive committee was formed on 1 April 1929 and the first SRA Handbook appeared in the 1929/30 season. 1930 was a year of many firsts, heralding the English Inter-Country Championship, the Inter-Services Championship, and most important of all, the first British Open.

Charles Read, professional at the Queen's Club in London was designated 'Open champion' but lost both legs of a challenge match against Don Butcher of London's Conservative Club who thus became the first winner of the event that was to be regarded as the unofficial world championship until 1976 and is still rated by many of the top players as the title to win. Butcher retained the title the following year when he defeated Charles Arnold but the 1930s really belonged to the man who beat him in 1932—Abel Fattah Amr.

With the victory the stylish Egyptian, who played his squash at Royal Automobile Club in Pall Mall, became the first man to win the British Amateur and British Open titles in the same season. In all he held six Amateur and six Open titles during the thirties including the 1933 Open in which he was unchallenged.

In Britain women's squash get developed in years 1932 to 1934. In 1932 the SRA appointed a committee to manage the women's game in this country and the following year a British women's team toured overseas for the first time when they visited North America where they won the Wolfe-Noel Cup, an event run intermittently until 1968. In 1934 the Women's Squash Rackets Association was founded and, like the SRA, not only took charge of the game in England but unofficially acted as governing body for international game. By 1932 62 clubs and organisations were affiliated to the SRA, together with 50 individuals, and Devonshire had formed the first county association.

In 1932 a squash ball cost I/6d, a racket about £1 and a brick and cement court could be built for less than £600. A court with a gallery and changing facilities would have been as much as £800. The game made great strides in England during the middle and later thirties with many competitions being started, and in 1937 the seeds were sown for the formation of a home international tournament when Scotland played both England and Ireland. Following a dispute with the SRA over the standard ball, the professionals formed a breakaway association but the argument was resolved just before the war and the two bodies merged. The growth of the game in 1930s is best illustrated by SRA's membership figures in 1939.

The first county association had only been formed in 1931, but at the outbreak of war the SRA had 32 countries within its membership, divided into 10 areas with a combined total of 320 clubs. Countries affiliated had risen from four in 1931 to include organisations from Ireland, Scotland, Wales, Australia, Egypt, India, New Zealand, South Africa, Hong Kong, Federated Malay States and China. However, not everything was rosy in the squash garden.

Towards the end of decade there were strong but unsuccessful moves, at various times, to introduce a faster ball, lower the tin by two inches, put holes or marks

just above the tin which, if hit, would give a player a bonus point, and place obstacles in certain places around the court—particularly in the back corners. Why were such radical changes being suggested? Many people felt that rallies were becoming too long and saw these as possible ways of shortening them.

As was suggested by criticism in the 1920s some things really do not change, bearing in mind the arguments that have raged from the mid seventies onwards concerning the ball and long, boring matches. After the growth of 1930s, squash, like every other sport, suffered harshly from the rigours of the Second World War. Many buildings in London has been damaged or destroyed and squash balls were in very short supply and or of poor quality. The Bath Club was one of those damaged and the 1946 British Amateur had to move to the Lansdowne Club. It was this competition more than most that brought home the stark reality of what had gone on in the previous six years.

Missing from field of 90 were the only three men other than the great Amr to win the championship in the thirties—Victor Cazalet, Cyril Hamilton and Kenneth Gandar Dower, the last champion before the war. All had been killed in action. As the game got under way again, Norman Borrett, currently president of the English SRA, registered the first of his five successive victories, while Jim Dear, who had finally won the Open title in 1938/9 season after being runner-up three times, lost the first post-was championship to Mahmoud Karim. This was the last British Open played on the challenge system but the new knock-out format seemed to make little difference as the same two fought out the next year's final with the same result.

Till late forties building restrictions was in force which prevented the growth of game, it was estimated that some 200,000 people were visiting the 300 clubs still in use throughout Britain. It seemed certain that a boom would come as soon as restricted were lifted. But the boom was not destined to arrive, in England at any rate, until the late 1960s by which time squash had already become an overwhelmingly popular public sport. in Australia.

Curtain raisers to the squash growth were undoubtedly the Khans with their dominance of the world's major events in the 1950s. Their skills inspired many to the sport and the eventual arrival of a home-grown hero in form of Jonah Barrington in the mid sixties was just the catalyst that British squash needed. Barrington's feats, his ability to sell himself and the game and his rivalry with Australian Geoff Hunt ushered in the era of professionalism as court building in Britain got under way and at a speed that no one would have believed possible in the depressing post-was years.

The success of commercial squash court operations in Australia was mirrored in Britain as land and money became available and the sport's inherent appeal of brisk exercise in pleasant surroundings triggered a surge of court development that was to last from the late sixties to the end of the next decade. This in turn fuelled interest in the continent of Europe where the sport is steadily gaining a foothold in many countries, particularly in Germany where the expansion rate has been phenomenal.

Elsewhere in the world, squash continues to expand, notably in south-east Asia where Singapore leads the way with an almost fanatical enthusiasm. Not surprisingly, membership of the International Squash Rackets Federation, founded in 1967, has grown from a handful of countries to the present state of more than 50 members.

The ISRF took over control of the sport from the SRA in the year of their formation and is now the body responsible for implementing and changing the rules. The professional game has prospered too with the International Squash Players Association being formed in 1973 and now looking after the interests of more than 100 members.

A Women's Players Association was formed in April 1984. The men's squash game did not go Open until 1980, but by the mid seventies the amateur who could survive with the pro's at the highest level was a dying breed. The Women's Squash Rackets Association had already approved Open competition in 1973, so in many ways they were more far-sighted than the men in anticipating future trends in squash. In 1977 plans were revealed in England for a four wall glass squash court and although it took several years before such a court appeared, the announcement sparked the movement towards spectator squash.

Such development could possibly bring about radical changes within squash since spectator squash is not merely about people watching but about providing entertainment and this could mean permanent rule changes, new scoring and a different ball. Squash is feeling the effect of the need to sell itself via television and as the sport approaches 21st century there could be spectacular developments in store.

DOUBLES GAME

Doubles has long been played in North America—their first national championship began in 1933 and its popularity there has been aided by specially built courts.

In England, the game barely survives, owing existence to its appeal as a fun event rather than a competition of a serious nature, although having said that, the women's SRA have run a Double Cup since 1957 and in February 1984 a British national doubles championship for both men and women was played at South Marston Country Club, Swindon in Wilsthire. This was the first time there had been a British men's doubles championship at either national or international level. The men's event was won by Christy Willstrop and Bob Forde and the women by Karen Butterworth and Nicola Spurgeon.

The main difference between squash and other court games is that it has developed almost exclusively as a singles game, and looking at the size of the singles court it is easy to see why. The lack of space for 4 active players prevents a fluid game developing and there is also the high probability that unless extreme caution is exercised someone will be struck with either a ball or racket or both. The standard dimensions of a double court 45 ft. long by 25 ft wide, as opposed to singles court dimensions 32 ft × 21 ft, are the same as those accepted by the United States SRA so any effort to eventually draw together the two codes could find immediate common ground in doubles. The first doubles court in England is believed to have been at Prince's Club and this was not of standard size.

Susan Noel, British women's Open champion 1932-34, writing in her book Sports Women's Manual, thinks the Prince's court had been improvised from an old rackets court or some similar disused playing area.

However, she recalls that the members treated the game seriously and frequently arranged tournaments. This use continued until the club closed down in 1939.

Miss Noel thinks that the doubles game in Britain owned more to the taste for doubles acquired by English women's teams touring America during 1930s. In 1935 Miss Lytton Milbanke and Mrs. McKechnie won the women's national doubles title in the United States and in 1936 the same partnership proved successful in a women's Open event held at Prince's. Other women who toured abroad also became interested and Susan Noel has no doubt that it was the influence of these players which resulted in the construction of standard doubles courts, built to American specifications, at the Ladies Carlton Club, the St. Johns Wood Squash Rackets Club and the Edinburgh Club.

These three above mentioned courts, together with the non-standard Prince's were the only courts in Britain and unhappily the only one now remaining is at Edinburgh since after the closure of Prince's, as in Second World War other 2 courts got destroyed.

3

COURT

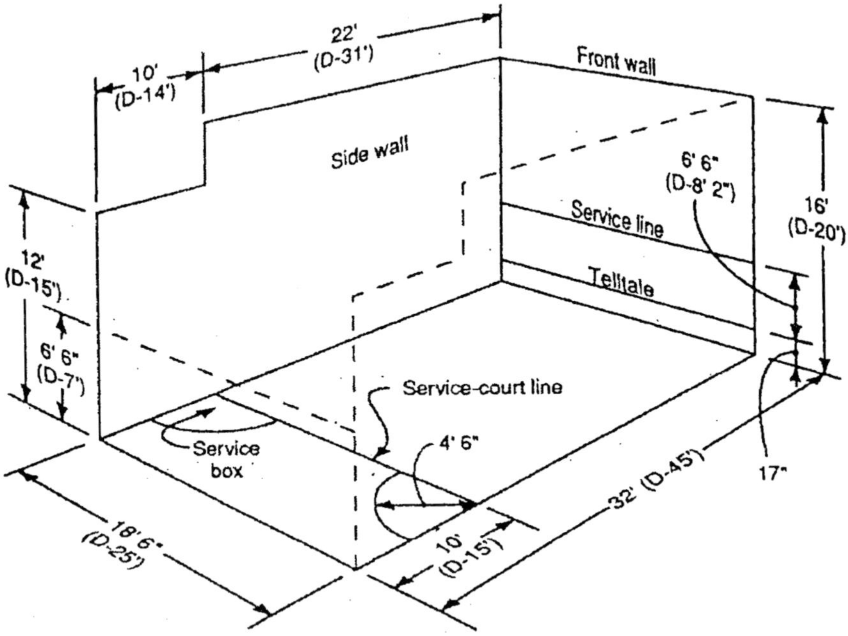
22'
(D-31')
10'
(D-14')
Front wall
Side wall
6' 6"
(D-8' 2")
Service line
16'
(D-20')
Telltale
12'
(D-15')
6' 6"
(D-7')
Service-court line
Service
box
4' 6"
17"
32' (D-45')
18' 6"
(D-25')
10'
(D-15')

If you have not seen a squash court, imagine a large yet claustrophobic prison cell bounded by high white walls, with the only escape route a flush-fitting door merging into the back wall. Or imagine a pit-constructed above ground level instead of below it. To enjoy the full flavour of the setting, and the fact that squash is the only popular "racket" or "court" game in which both players are on the same side of the "net"- which in squash consists of what is known as the tin, or board. The close proximity of two fast-moving players, swinging rackets, underlines the importance of keeping out of each other's way. The diagram gives you a more detailed idea of the court's appearance and dimensions.

Now for a few notes on the various boundaries of the court, starting at the top. When you step onto a strange court, take a good look at the height of the roof and the arrangement of the various fittings beneath it. If you absorb the lessons you read there, there can be no excuse for indiscreet use-or neglect- of the lob. There is no standard height for the roof, and no standard colour, A low roof means that you would be a fool to rely on tactical use of the lob; a high roof gives you more scope. As for colours, there are some courts with dark roofs, which make the flight of the ball difficult to follow up there. Given a high, dark roof, you can cause your opponent a lot of trouble by lobbing. The position of the lighting fixtures and any beams or guiders will also affect your use of the lob. Lighting systems very. The traditional arrangement consists of six lamp, three on either side of the court, the two front lamps having reflectors to direct the light onto the front wall. Nowadays there is a move towards fluorescent strip lighting . This has aroused mixed feelings because the "cold " white light it provides differs in quality from that supplied by the traditional lamps. But fluorescent lighting, more expensive to install but cheaper to run, is gradually

becoming accepted Outside courts have glass roofs, so you can play by daylight. If the various fixtures in the roof are unusual, ask if the club have any "local rules" governing match play. What we are saying in all these notes about the roof is simply this: adapt your game to the court.

The plastered walls are usually white or off-white- occasionally apple green, which is restful for the eyes. The walls are affected by humidity, and a sudden change in temperature can make them sweat. In these conditions the geometry of the game goes haywire, because the ball skids off the walls instead of rebounding at the usual angles. When you notice condensation, hit low and hard, and forget about the clever stuff. A sweating court tends to make the floor slippery, too, so that your footwork, like your strokes, has to be more inhibited than usual. As for the door, this is made of thick teak to give the ball the same rebound as the walls. The tin stretching across the bottom of the front wall is made of a resounding material, such as zinc. The play line at the top of the tin protrudes from the wall and is sometimes angled, to deflect the flight of any shot that hits it.

The best floors are laid like the floor of a dance hall that is to say, sprung. This eliminates jarring, helps the player to move about, and, in general, saves the feet some were and tear. Canadian maple is often used because of its hardness and its light colour.

In adapting your tactics to the court, the most influential factor is temperature. A warm court means a faster game, with lots of bounce in the ball and the emphasis on concentration, stamina, and accuracy. The rallies are long. The stroke player is at a disadvantage. Indoor courts are warm-very warm if they happen to be close to a heated swimming pool, or to kitchens. Most of the big championships are played on courts like this, so that players from the provinces start with the tactical handicap of having to play a type of game to which they are not accustomed. On cold courts the ball does not bounce much. It travels more slowly and dies more quickly. In these conditions the stroke player can show us all his tricks. Courts that stand out in the open are usually cold. Right from the start you should learn to recognize and exploit- the difference between hot and cold courts.

4

THE LANGUAGE OF THE GAME

Any instructional book fall short of its aims if the terms used are not fully explained. This is particularly relevant to a book on squash, which has a vocabulary appropriate to the game's unique and abundant pleasures. The glossary given here is as comprehensive as we can make it, with two reservations: first, we have not included the words for describing the various parts of the court and second, we give here only the briefs definitions of words explained in detail elsewhere in the book. That language is ounce will put you, as it were three points up- {1} You will know more about the game; {2} You will know what you are talking about; and {3} When you discuss the game, or play it, with someone less well versed in the grammar of squash, you will be able to blind him with science! After all, psychological warfare is all part of the fun of the game.

Ace

Term sometimes used to describe an outright service winner- that is, a service which the receiver is unable to return.

Angle

This is an attacking shot played onto the side wall the striker is facing. The ball then ricochets from the side wall to the front wall. The shot can be used for two purposes- one, to get your opponent out of position; two, to make a winner if he is already out of position. Angles can also be referred to as "good lengths" if they die before rebounding from the opposite side wall.

Reverse Angle

A similar shot, but played across court- onto the wall to which the striker has his back turned. For example, if the striker plays a backhand stroke, hitting the ball onto the right-hand side wall, this is a reverse angle.

Appeal

A player may appeal against the marker's decision, which may then be reconsidered by the referee or by the marker himself if he is in sole charge of the match.

Backhand

A stroke played on the striker's left-hand side, the head of the racket moving from the vicinity of the left shoulder and following through beyond the right shoulder.

Backhand Court

The left-hand side of the court.

Boost

A defensive stroke forced upon a player when the ball is returned to such an awkward position that usually he can only make a return by first playing the ball onto a side wall or the back wall. **Back- wall boast-** A boast off the back wall. **Double boast-** In this case the ball hits both side walls before striking the front wall. For all types of boast.

Check

Many players try to keep up a pretty fast pace, with the aim of beating an opponent by speed. But by checking the stroke immediately before hitting the ball, the striker can unexpectedly slow down his return. This sudden variation in pace can catch the opponent flat-footed, or make him mistime his stroke by striking too soon.

Clinger

A shot that travels straight back down the nearest side wall and clings to it. Basically a negative shot, but tactically useful, since it is difficult to return and cannot be attacked. In returning it, do not take a full swing: be satisfied to scrape the ball carefully off the wall with a relaxed grip, letting the wrist do the work.

Crowding

A player is said to be crowding his opponent when he stands or moves so close that the opponent's freedom of stroke or movement is restricted.

Cut

This is severe backspin, which is applied to the ball in order to bring it down sharply as soon as it has hit the front wall.

Cut service

The application of cut when serving, to bring the ball down steeply on a good length, or to attempt a nick.

Die

The ball is said to die when it loses all its impetus and trickles so close to the floor and a well that it cannot be returned. This is usually achieved by directing the ball into the nick, or very close to it, after applying cut or slice to the stroke.

Drop Shot

Usually played from the front of the court, this is a gently hit stroke, with cut, intended to die in the nick close to one of the front corners.

Fair View

A service that contravenes the Rules. Foot fault-occurs if the server, in the act of striking the ball, has not got at least one foot on the floor and within the line marking the service box. Fox all faults.

Follow-through

In squash, as in most ball games, an important part of every stroke occurs after impact. The completion of the swing is called the follow-through.

Forehand

Stroke played on the striker's right-hand side, the head of the racket moving from the vicinity of the right shoulder and following through beyond the left shoulder. **Forehand court**- The right-hand side of the court.

Gallery

Accommodation for spectators, providing a view over the back wall and, on some championship courts, over the side walls. The gallery of a squash court provides a similar view- though much closer to the action- to the gallery of a theatre.

Game

The first player to win nine points wins a game, except that on the first call of " eight-all" hand-out may, if he chooses, set the game to two: this means that the first player to score two more points win the game.

Game Ball

When the server needs one points to win the game. There is no call of "match point" in squash: when a match reaches this stage, the call is still "game ball"

Half-Volley

Stroke played neither before nor after the bounce, but while the ball is still in contact with the floor.

Hand

The period of play from the time a player becomes server until he becomes receiver **Hand out**- The player who is serving

Kill

A heavily cut stroke that "kill" the ball and makes it impossible to retrieve. Kills are usually achieved by hard hits into the nick of the barest side wall. An the highest level slim players hit the ball so hard that they can occasionally kill it with out using the nick. What happens here is that a powerful and well timed shot takes all the resilience out of the soft ball so that, as if punctured, it dies on leaving the front wall.

Knock-up

A period of five minutes, before a match, in which players are allowed to practice on court.

Length

This describes a stroke that hits the ball straight up and down a side wall- or across court- at such a pace that the ball dies in a back corner after the first bounce. It may fail to reach the back wall, or may reach it only to drop sharply and die, instead of rebounding.

Let

An undecided rally, which is played again. Common causes of lets are: a doubtful return; the denial of a fair view; a player hit by the ball or a racket; a player's inability to play a proper stroke because his opponent is crowding him; and obstruction of the striker as he tries to get to the ball.

Lob

A stroke that sends the ball soaring over the opponent to drop into the back of the court. **Lob service**- The lob used as a service.

Maker

An official appointed to control a match and call the score. If no referee is appointed, the marker exercises the referee's power as well as his own.

Masking

A technique vital to successful tactics, since it is the basis of deception. A player can mask his intentions by a sudden turn of the wrist just before impact, thus playing a drop shot or angle when a good length is expected, or vice versa. The opponent is caught on the wrong foot or persuaded to move the wrong way. The Egyptians, who have particularly good wrists, are adept at masking.

Match

Consists of the best of three or five games.

Nick

The junction of walls and floor. Also describes a shot that goes into the nick and therefore bounces unpredictably **Dead nick**- This occurs when the ball lands full in the nick and, instead of bouncing, rolls along the floor and is therefore unpayable. Obviously a useful shot to play, though it demands great accuracy- or luck !

Not up

Called by the maker when the ball is struck on its second bounce, or when the ball is not returned above the board in accordance with the rules. The striker loses the rally.

Opening up the Court

Tactical process of playing stroke that forces the opponent into a corner, so that almost the entire court is left open for a winner.

Out of Court

Called by the marker when the ball touches any part of the walls outside the playing area, or touches or passes over any beams, girders, or light in the roof of the court. The lines marking the upper limits of the playing area are themselves out of court.

Penalty Point

Usually awarded only at the game's higher levels; this is more severe penalty than a let. It means that- the offending player loses the hand or loses a point. A common cause for the award of a penalty point; when a player fails to give his opponent a fair view of the ball and freedom of stroke.

Play

Called by the marker if a service is good, if a fault is play by the receiver, or if the marker considers a rally should continue in spite of a doubtful stroke.

Pull

When positioned for a normal forehand or backhand drive, a player may fox his opponent with a pull instead of playing straight, and hitting the ball when it alongside him, the striker takes the ball in advance, slightly in front of him. This puts the striker's body between the ball and his opponent, who is temporarily unsighted, and it also means that the ball is hit across court, instead of up and down the nearest side wall as the receiver expects. The stroke begins farther than usual from the shoulder of the racket arm. Its aim is to catch the opponent on the wrong foot or make him move the wrong way.

Put out

A player who is hand-in is said to be " put out" when he lose a rally.

Rally

The continuous exchange of shots between the service and the moment when hand-in either scores a point or becomes handout.

Receiver

At the beginning of a rally, handout is the receiver. Afterwards, receiver" denotes the player who has to make the next stroke but one.

Referee

An additional official, usually an amateur, who is appointed at important championships to assist the marker and adjudicate on tricky decisions. The referee awards lets or penalty points. A player may appeal to the referee to reconsider decisions made by the maker. The referee deals with all appeals.

Set

It is part of the marker's job to remind handout that the score in 8-all and that hand -out must make a choice before the next service. Handout may decide to play the best of three points , which means that the player winning the next point wins the game. The usual choice is "set two" which hand-out may indicate to the marker by raising two fingers so a game cannot to farther than 10-9

Slice

A stroke that puts clockwise spin on the ball. A sliced backhand makes the ball spin anticlockwise. In each case, the are of the swing and the position of the racked head differ from the normal stroke. The effect is to make the ball shoot away from the striker at a much greater angle than usual.

Smash

A full-blooded volley, played with the head of the racket above shoulder height. If you can make the ball rebound from the front wall into the nick, your opponent will be confounded by the angle of the shot as well as its speed. He may even be beaten by an outright kill. But in squash, as in tennis, a genuine smash can only be played safely from the front half of the court.

Side-wall Smash

Played onto the side wall, this is really a violent version of the angle.

Striker

The player whose turn it is to hit the ball.

Time

Called by the marker when he wishes to stop play. The marker also calls " Time" after the five minutes allowed for the knock-up; and after the permitted interval between games.

Turning

This usually occurs when the ball rebounds so awkwardly from side wall to back wall that it cannot be returned in the conventional way. So the striker turns round anticlockwise in the wise in the backhand corner, following the ball, in the forehand corner, in order to played backhand.

Volley

Stroke played before the ball has bounced. **Drop Volley**- drop shot played before the ball has bounced.

5

THE GRIP

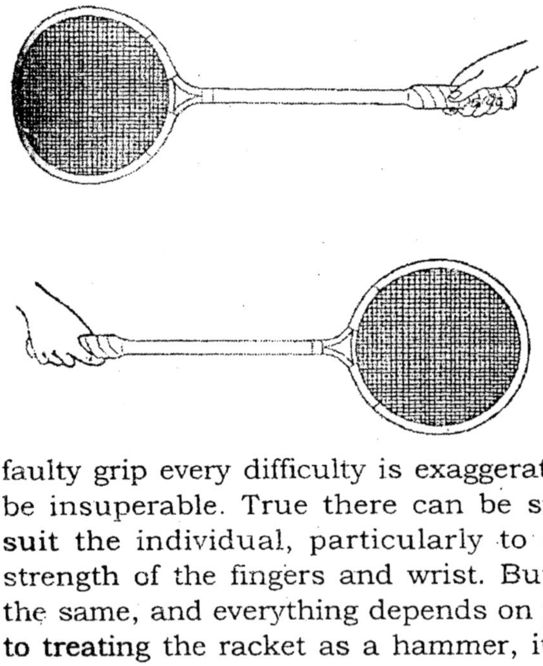

When you come to think about it, the way you grip the racket is the basis of all your game's virtues -of all its vices. With the right grip, you can master each of the game's techniques in turn. With a faulty grip every difficulty is exaggerated and some may be insuperable. True there can be small variations to suit the individual, particularly to suit the size and strength of the fingers and wrist. But the basic grip is the same, and everything depends on it. If you get used to treating the racket as a hammer, it will be a difficult business changing to the correct grip later on- as you will have to, if you are going to improve. So start off on the right foot, or in this case, the right grip. If you can check it with a professional, so much the better: he will spot a flaw instantly.

There is a simple method of finding the right grip. Open the hand, with the palm upwards, and slightly spread the fingers. With the head of the racket horizontal, put the handle into the palm of your hand, so that the butt rests on the heel of the hand and slants across the palm between the thumb and forefinger. Now grip the handle by closing round it the second, third, and fourth fingers. Curl the forefinger round the handle, too, but slightly away from the other fingers, so that it will stretch farther along the handle. The thumb curls round the handle as if to join the forefinger, but does not touch it. Do not let the thumb lie uselessly along the handle- it must curl round the handle. Now examine the grip and let us see how it works. The tip of the little finger should be at least ¾ in. From the end of the handle. The three fingers tucked in together give you a firm grip and allow your wrist freedom of movement. The thumb and forefinger guide and control the racket so that you can place the ball accurately, and also act as support when you hit hard, or volley.

The grip is the same for backhand and forehand, though the position of the wrist is obviously different because you have to keep the face of the racket " open" On the forehand this means that the back of your hand faces to your right. On the forehand you turn the wrist so that the back of your hand faces upwards. But the grip itself does not change. Only the wrist.

Squash is such a fast game that you have no time to adjust your grip. If you do adjust it, you're in trouble: for one thing, the ball comes to you so quickly that changing the grip invites technical errors; for another, your concentration will be momentarily diverted from the ball. Once you start messing about like this, you will throw points away or keep on apologizing for hitting lucky returns off the wood.

One of the basic principles of a good grip is that it allows complete freedom for using the wrist. This is very important. In tennis, power comes from a "locked" wrist and a long swing. But a long swing in squash in dangerous and therefore penalized. So the power has to come from a sudden lash of the wrist. Get this into your head from the start and you will not only be a good player will be a safe player, too. A flexible wrist gives you power plus safety, and variety plus deception.

Now for those small variations we mentioned at the start of the chapter. They concern "long" and "short" grips. The long grip-the one we have taught you-has the little finger near the very end of the handle. The short of the racket.

The long grip gives you a more extensive reach more power. But if it is too long, the head of the racket may feel unwieldy and the wrist will therefore lose some of its control over the stroke. The short grip gives you more control, a better "feel" of the ball. But it reduces both reach and power. All right, you say, what am I to do? The aim is to find a compromise that will suit the size and strength of your wrist and fingers. Try a long grip first. Then experiment a bit to find the position that feels most comfortable. Remember that control over the ball is vital. If you have a small hand and a weak wrist, a shorter grip might be best but don't overdo it at the expense of your reach. Finally, having found the position that suits you, cultivate it and stick to it. This position should never be adjusted during the course of a rally.

6

FOOTWORK

The thing about footwork in squash is that in a confined area you have five moving bodies- two players, two rackets, and a ball. All these are carving their way through the air at all sorts of speeds and angles. Your job is to make your opponent hurtle about like a madman while you keep out of his way and get into position to play your own strokes. In these circumstances the cricket professional's advice to young batsmen is hardly sufficient for our purpose. We shall discuss footwork more fully in dealing with each stroke, but meantime there are a few important general principles you should master. These mostly spring from the prime need for speed-off the mark, and in turning. In acquiring the necessary agility you have to "dance" rather than run; to take more short steps than big strides; to glide rather than bound. Keep your feet reasonably close together, because this will make it easier for you to turn quickly, neatly, and in balance, instead of lunging awkwardly. During a rally your knees should always be slightly bent, your weight slightly forward and on the balls or toes of your feet, not the heels.

And you should keep moving- this is less exhausting than " stop go" methods. While the ball is buzzing about you will never have time to stand still, because after every shot you play there are two urgent jobs to do: getting back to the centre of the court so that you are in position and facing the front wall, and keeping your eyes on the ball.

There is a perfect position for every stroke- a perfect place to go, a perfectly balanced arrangement of feet, body, arms, and racket. Always aim for this perfection. You will not always have time to achieve it, but the harder you try, to more chance you will have of playing the stroke you want to play. You can play off the " wrong" foot deliberately, to confuse your opponent, but this is advanced stuff-learn how to do thing right before you experiment with doing them wrong. To sum up, remember that to play a controlled stroke you have to be properly balanced; that to be properly balanced you have to be in position with time to spare; that to be in position with time to spare, you need anticipation and speed off the mark. Work on it- and in time you will cover the court with flowing ease and instinctive assurance.

7

FOREHAND

The forehand is a natural stroke and should not be complicated by too much theory. All we are trying to do here is to help you play it with maximum efficiency on a squash court. This is merely a question of arranging yourself, and your racket, in the most balanced and effective way- in relation, of course, to the position of the ball. Regard these notes as snippets of good advice, rather than a routine to be learnt parrot fashion. Perhaps the best way to set about it is to split the stroke into its three separate components preparation, impact, and follow-through. Remember that you are playing a simple, straightforward stroke. The ball is coming down the right-hand side wall. You want to intercept the ball at the moment when an imaginary line between your left foot, the ball, and the side wall will from a right-angle with that wall. Your aim is to smack the ball hard and low onto the front wall so that it will come back straight and low down the side wall to a good length. Here we go then.

Preparation

Turn to face the side wall and put your left foot forward, parallel with the front wall. Knee slightly bent. Toes pointing straight at the side wall. As the ball approaches and that left foot goes firmly down, with your weight on it, two other things should happen-left shoulder down and racket back and up in a line parallel

with the side wall. Elbow bent. The head of the racket is not in line with the forearm, because the wrist is bent upwards and backwards -" cocked". By doing this you will get maximum " whip" on your shot. Get down to it. Tuck your stomach in. Right you are properly poised, like a tiger ready to pounce on his lunch... You are watching the ball every inch of the way.

Impact

Don't let the ball pass you before impact. The ideal spot for the explosion is about 9 in. from the floor and about 2ft. from the left foot, bang in line between left shoulder, left foot, and side wall. Lean into the shot. Swing low, but keep the head of the racket up and its face " open". The position of the feet- and the are of the swing in relation to the feet-is not unlike that of a straight drive played off the front foot in cricket. Don't play the stroke too close to the body, or you will be cramped. On impact, your shoulders are parallel with the side wall, your body perfectly balanced and so still that you could be posing for a picture: at that moment, all the action is concentrated in racket, wrist, and arms.

Follow-through

As you hit the ball, the racket follows through, up over the left shoulder in line with the path of the ball. Your forearm finishes close to the body, your hand just below the left shoulder. You have hit a superb shot. But you do not stand there and admire it. Immediately after impact you are already " pushing off" to hurry back to the middle of the court. You are still watching the ball. You are ready to give your next demonstration of perfect stroke play: preparation, impact, and follow-through.

But be will assume that, on occasion, you share with every other human being the capacity for error. The important thing is to be constructive in your exasperation, to work out why you made the mistake. Here are a few clues to help your investigations. You hit down? Well perhaps you were late in your preparations, in getting the racket back. Perhaps you failed to keep the face of the racket "open". *Maybe you hit the ball to high.* This could happen because you struck the ball too soon-while the racket was rising, towards the end of the swing. Or because your weight was on the wrong foot. *Perhaps your direction was at fault.* Clumsy footwork might be the cause. If you plant your left foot too far across towards the side wall, consider the implication: as the ball rebounds from the front wall it will be heading straight for your left leg, instead of for the gap between left leg and side wall. You cannot let the ball hit you. Nor do you want to play a cramped shot that may leave a dent in your shinbone. So bad footwork forces you to play the ball too soon- while it is between your left leg and the front wall. Your swing will go round the leg instead of parallel with the side wall, and the ball will go across court instead of down the right-hand side wall: Equally, you might send the ball in the wrong direction because you hit it too late, letting it pass you before impact: in this case the ball goes onto the side wall first, instead of the front wall, and finishes in the middle of the court -a sitting duck for a grateful opponent. To avoid these misdirected shots, you must swing on the path you want the ball to follow. To do this, get your feet and body round to face the side wall, with your left foot beside the ball and your left shoulder down, over that left foot, before making contact. And crack the ball while it is between your left foot and the side wall.

All these are specific cause of specific errors. There are a few general points to bear in mind, too. Perhaps you were too close to the ball when you hit it. Perhaps you failed to keep your body still at the moment of impact. Perhaps you took your eye off the ball for a second. The overall lesson is this: think what you're doing concentrate.

8

BACKHAND

The same general principles apply to forehand and backhand alike, with the obvious proviso that everything happens the other way round-left becomes right, and so on. There are a few points demanding special emphasis when you play a backhand drive. The first is that, as this is a less "natural" stroke than the forehand, it is vital to get "setup" right, to have feet and body properly arranged. The second is that to keep the face of the racket "open" the wrist has to be turned so that, on the backhand, the back of the hand faces upwards. The third is that the backswing-the full backswing must be made in plenty of time a late start may tempt you to snatch at the ball and play a rather wild follow through, instead of using the orthodox swing. You cannot compensate for a late start. The forth is the follow through itself, which, on the backhand, can be highly dangerous. For the ordinary backhand drive, straight down the side wall, even as the racket starts rising at the end of its swing. The racket should finish almost vertical, between your right shoulder and the front wall. Never swing the follow through round the body so that the racket finishes pointing to the right-handside wall. Such a stroke would be {a} technically bad, {b} dangerous, an d {c} illegal,. In this respect a flexible wrist is blatantly important, because a locked wrist would invite a follow-through fraught with risk.

Make a point of getting your backhand right from the start of your squash career. The wall prevents you from "running round" a weak backhand, as some tennis players do. So you cannot afford weakness on that flank. In general, you should use it for all the shots you play on the left-hand side of the court, just as on the right' hand side you should use your forehand.

The clues we gave about rectifying mistakes on the advice we have just given about keeping the face of the racket "open", about the importance of the backswing and follow through. Most of all, remember that more often than not a bad backhand is due to bad footwork. You must get that right foot across, so that at the moment of impact the right foot is nearer than the left foot to the side wall. Your body has to be turned to the left in good time, so that your right shoulder comes down over your right foot before you hit the ball.

9

LENGTH

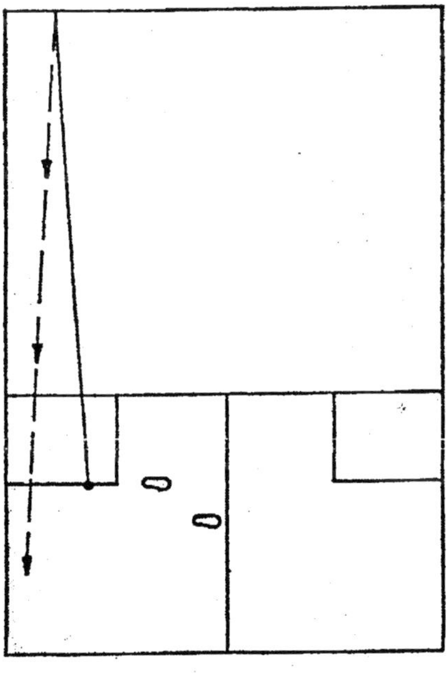

Competitive games are meaningless unless you play to win, In squash, as in tennis, there are three ways of doing this: hitting outright winners; forcing your opponent to make mistakes; or a combination of the two. In every case the basis of a winning game is the same- the ability to put your opponent on the defensive by hitting to a good length. You can hit hard and you can hit gently. You can hit straight up and down the nearest side wall, or you can hit across court. But if you go for a length with a gently hit cross-court stroke, this must obviously be a lob- or your opponent will intercept it. When we talk about length, we are primarily discussing a hard hit ball that

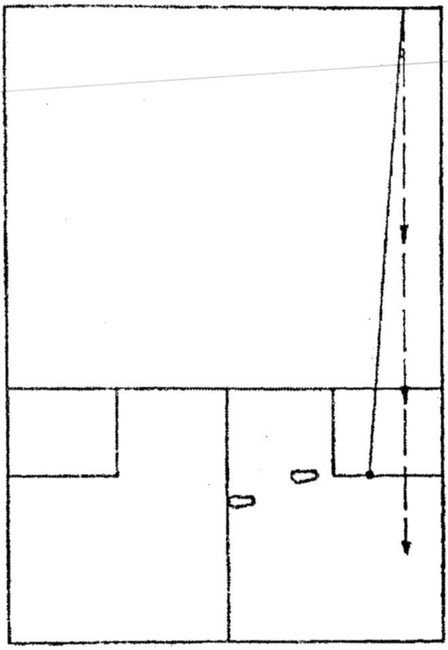

dies in one of the back corners after the first bounce-or is so close to death that the opponent has the devil of a job digging it out of the corner and making his return. If you strike a length, your opponent is continually in two minds- should he try to cut off the shot before it reaches the back of the court, or should he wait, in the hope that the ball rebound far enough for him to take a swing at it? Either way, this is defensive thinking- and you have forced it upon him. Either way, you have got him away from the middle of the court, which means that you are playing a successful tactical game.

In going for a length down the nearest side wall aim for a spot about 3 ft. above the tin and hit the ball hard enough to make it bounce in or close to the nick within two or three yards of the back wall. The point of the high clearance above the tin is that if you hit too low, the ball will bounce so far forward that your opponent will be able to intercept. To hit gently to a good length, obviously you must aim higher up the front wall. When you learn how to "cut" the ball this will help you to achieve a good length. As for the good length cross-court shots, these tend to be easier to intercept or retrieve, since they have farther to travel and, for much of the way, are well clear of the side walls. So use cross court shots sparingly.

Do Face the side wall. Play off the correct foot. Get your shoulder down. Lift the head of the racket above the level of the wrist. Bend the knee of the front leg. During the stroke, keep the body relaxed but still, the racket face open.

Keep your eye on the ball at all times.

Finally, as a good length is the basis of your game, make it your first priority as you adjust to the court and the ball during the knock-up and early in the match itself. If your opponent is anywhere near your own standard, them the first man to strike a length will gain the initiative.

Don't: Face the front wall. Play off the wrong foot. Stand too close to the ball. Let your shoulder come up. Stand upright Move your feet before the stroke is completed. Drop the head of the racket. Lift your head.

Note: The advice {"Do" and "Don't"} applies to both forehand and backhand.

10

SERVICE

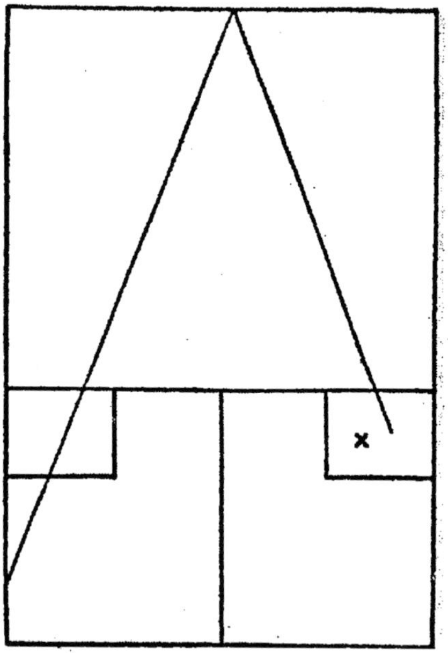

A service is not just a means of starting a rally. If you can put the ball in the right place at the right speed on the right line of flight, the initiative is your- because your opponent will have to play a defensive shot from a cramped position in one of the back corners. Occasionally you may even serve an outright winner- though this seldom happens at the game's highest level. A well directed service puts you momentarily in command. A badly directed service may enable your opponent to hit an immediate winner. In follows that you cannot expect to hit an outright winner with the service itself: the important thing is to get the ball safely into play and make thing awkward for the other chap. You cannot afford to be inaccurate. Nor is there any excuse for it, since the service is the one stroke you can play in your own time, without being hurried. All this may make you a little tense. Movement releases tension, so try walking two paces forward into your service action, making sure {a} that at least on foot lands in the service box, and {b} that your weight comes down onto the correct foot . At first, concentrate on serving forehand from both service boxes. When you can do this competently, develop a backhand service. This done, there is quite a lot of variety at your disposal. But first, the forehand service.

The rules demand that, when serving, you must have at least one foot on the floor within the service box and not touching the lines marking its boundaries. The ball must be hit directly onto the front wall above the cut line. Its first bounce must be in the opposite court, though the ball may hit the side wall or the back wall before it bounces.

Right. Let's get organized. Your stance at the moment of impact is the first thing to settle, because you will swing along a line parallel with an imaginary line from the toes of one foot to the toes of the other. You are serving forehand, remember . We will start in the right-hand box. As an experiment, adopt the same stance as that for the forehand drive, facing the side wall and hitting the ball when it is somewhere on the shortest line between your left foot and the right-hand side wall. But this time your body is upright and you hit the ball while it is at, or just below, eye level. Aim left for a spot about 3ft. above the cut line. The ball will than rebound down the middle of the court. If it lands in your own service court, it is a fault. If it lands in your opponent's, will murder it. So you have to adjust your angle, aiming nearer the middle of the front wall.

The pace and yard of the service depend on your service action. The direction of the service depends on

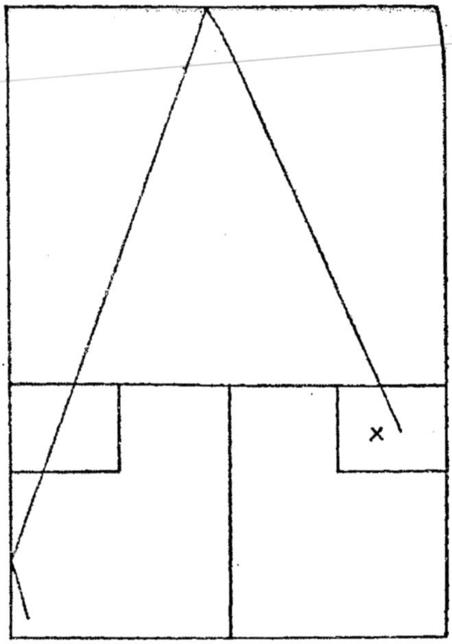

your stance. You will probably find the best stance brings you facing the vicinity of the front right-hand corner. But experiment until you get it right. And aim for a particular spot on the front wall: this will most likely be about 3ft. above the cut line, depending on how hard you hit. Always aim low at the beginning of the first game, until you get your eye in . Them gradually go higher.

Now move over to the left-hand service box and, still serving forehand, go through the same routine. The difference now is that, in turning your stance to achieve the best angle, you turn to the right-away from the front wall, instead of towards it. Again, practice until you can serve onto the side wall to a good length-whichever box you use, this service will give you the freedom of the court, because your opponent will be pained awkwardly in a back corner and forced to play a cramped return. Whether he volleys, boasts, or manages to organize some sort of drive, your next shot will not be difficult- because your good service has made him play a defensive and possibly tame stroke.

Whichever box you are serving from, you now have a businesslike forehand service at your disposal. The next thing you need is a backhand service, and this is trickier because -after getting the racket back- you have to toss the ball up under your right forearm. This takes some practice, but it is necessary. After all, the most consistent of services loses some of its value if your opponent always knows what is coming. He can learn how to deal with it. So variety is important. You have to be able to serve forehand or backhand, whichever suits your purposes best. Incidentally, you will notice that when serving backhand from the right-hand box, you have a full view of the court and, after serving, can step easily forward into that vital tactical position, the middle of the court. But the big thing about the two types of service is the variation in angle. By serving backhand from the right-hand box, and forehand from the left-hand box, and standing as near the middle of the court as possible, you can narrow the angle of the service and hit the ball down the side wall to a good length.

The best service of all is probably the slow lob. You hit this underarm, making the impact at about chest level, so that the ball is still rising as it hits the front wall about 8ft. above the cut line. Then it soars over your opponent and drops sharply to die in the back corner. If possible, it should brush the side wall a few inches below the out of court line-but don't hit this or you lose the rally . When using the lob service, stand well forward: when serving from the right-hand box, for instance, you many even have your left foot in the forecourt. This is a particularly effective service on slow courts, in which

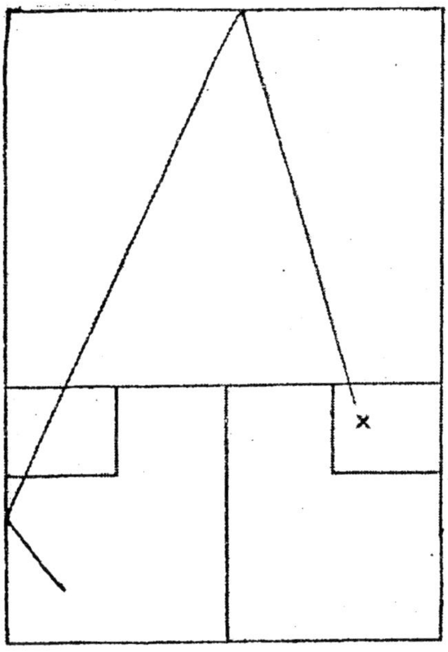

the ball tends to die in the back corners. It is a difficult service to volley properly, because of its high trajectory and its nearness to the side wall. And if your opponent fails so scrape back a volley, he will find the ball horribly awkward to dig out of the back corner. Another advantage, especially in a long and hard match, is that the lob service makes little demand on the server's physical strength. But it is less effective on a fast court and can you points on a court with a lob ceiling. If the court is sweating, avoid the lob altogether, because the ball is likely to skid straight off the front wall and fly up among the light fittings.

Other varieties of service are mostly throwbacks to the days when our ancestors knocked one another about with clubs. In squash terms, the equivalent is a hard hit overarm service, with the face of the racket vertical and the action similar to that a lawn tennis service. The ball should be directed lower than usual, just above the cut line, Aim for a rebound into the nick, or onto your opponent's toes-or belt the ball so hard that it cannons off the back wall and whizzes up the front of the court. You can even hammer the ball straight down the middle of the court. But all these violent services use up a lot of energy, and can be easy to return.

11

ANGLE

The walls give squash some attractive special qualities. One is obvious: they stop the ball getting out, at the end of a rally no one has to go ball-hunting, because it is never far away. But besides keeping the roof up and the ball within reach, the side the walls have other, more rewarding uses. They give squash an inimitable and engrossing character and play important roles in the battle of wits the game provides- because rebounds make possible all sorts of subtle, high-speed geometry in both attack and defence. At first the angles at which the ball flies about will be confusing, because you cannot relate them to any other game you have played.

There are three recognized side-wall shots-the angle, the reverse angle, and the boast. The first two are attacking shots, the third defensive. We will deal with the angle first. Though its purpose is offensive, its nature is delicate rather than violent. The travels from your racket onto the nearest side wall, rebounding to and from the front wall, to die near the farthest side wall.

Otherwise your opponent will have time to "read" and anticipate the shot and you will have to go out of his way, putting yourself out of position on the process. Experiment with your stance, and with the strength and lift of the stroke. Get your touch adjusted so that the ball dies where you want it to.

Your stance is like that for the ordinary drive, though the body and feet are turned slightly more away from the front wall. Save for this small variation, the stroke is the ordinary forehand or backhand drive, with the wrist open and the head of the racket up. Swing on a line parallel with the imaginary line from the toes of one foot to the toes of the other.

The angle can have either to two basic purposes. One is to manoeuvre you opponent out of position. The other is to make a winner when he is already out of position-behind you or backing hastily in that direction after he has played a shot from the front of the court. For example, when you have forced your opponent to boast, an angle in one way of exploiting the advantage thus gained. It then comes into its own as a surprise item. The position and stance from which you play it may lead your opponent to expect a drive to a length, a lob or a straight drop shot for the nearest front corner. The angle offers you yet another choice-another way to catch your man unprepared, and moving the wrong way. Its effect is much the same as that of the drop shot: to bring your opponent racing up to the front of the court.

Its advantage over the drop shot is that it is more likely to catch your opponent on the wrong foot: as he heads for one front corner, anticipating a drop shot, your angle towards the other front corner may even catch him cross-legged... Besides costing him the rally, this will do his morale no good at all.

12

REVERSE ANGLE

This is hit across court to the farthest side well, rebounding to and from the front wall, to die near the side wall from which you are playing the shot. Like the angle, it is a surprise item which can lure your opponent out of position, or catch him on the wrong foot and make you a winner-if the shot is played accurately. The reverse angle is sometimes used in returning a poor service. It is then an effective way of getting your opponent away from the middle of the court: moreover, it will put him on edge, because he will have to let the ball come across the court, in front of him, before he sets off to pursue it to the far side of the court. In other words, be will start late. This illustrates the difference between expectation and anticipation. If your opponent hits a poor service he may expect a reverse angle but he cannot anticipate it, because if he moves before the ball goes across him, he will move straight into its path and risk getting perforated. The reverse angle should not be attempted when your opponent is in the front of the court, unless he is hurrying backwards. The position of the ball at impact is important and-compared with almost every other stroke in the game-unusual. Because the ball is between you body and the front wall, not the side wall. At the moment of impact the line between your front foot, the ball, and the front wall is parallel with the side wall. When you practise the shot it will be obvious why you have take the ball in this position. It will also be obvious that you are playing across the line of flight; that hitting the opposite side wall takes so much speed off the ball that it may go down before reaching the front wall; that is these circumstances it would be optimistic to expect consistent accuracy; and that the reverse angle is therefore a stroke to use sparingly. It is, as it were, one of the luxuries of the game rather than a " bread and butter" shot. For all that, make the stroke part of your repertory. Take care in playing it. At the top of the backswing the head of the racket should be about shoulder high, its face "open ". Get your shoulder and body well down towards the ball before impact- and keep your body still as you hit the ball.

13

BOAST

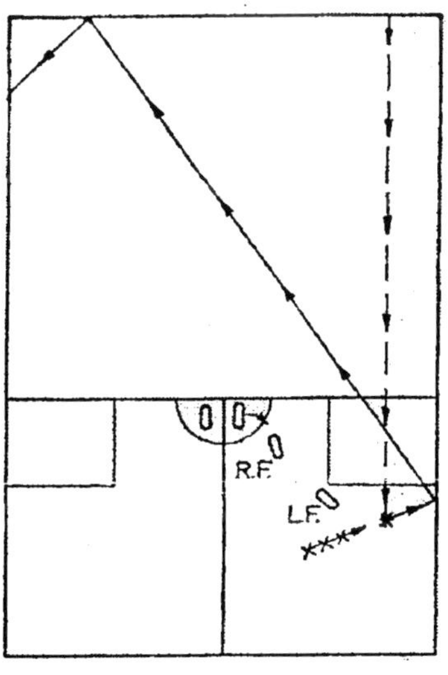

A competent opponent will explore the back comes persistently, especially when he is serving. So you will often have to hit the ball while it is covering about between you and a back corner- while the front wall is out of sight. In this situation you cannot play the ball direct onto the front wall. You should not even try to do so. Have the discretion to admit that a boast, a defensive shot, has been forced upon you. It is the only way to dig otherwise irretrievable shots out of the back corner. Often you will have to look sharp to achieve even a boast, though when receiving service you will be handily placed to get into position for the stroke. The shot comes in three varieties-single boast, double boast, and back-wall boast. By far the most frequent is the

Single boast

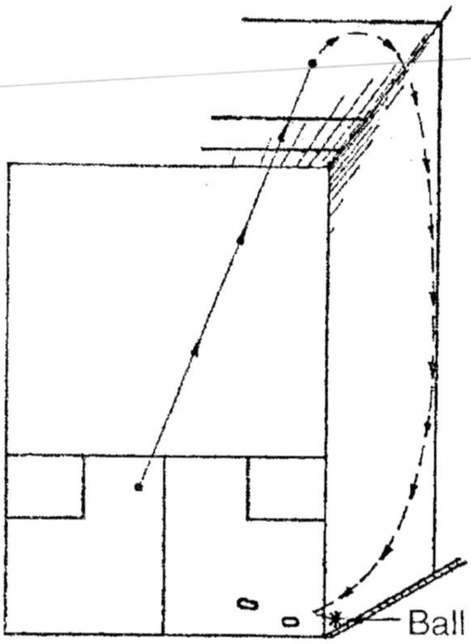

This is almost an angle shot in its direction, though it is played from farther back in the court. The ball is hit hard, upwards, onto the nearest side wall, rebounding across the court onto the front wall, then falling to die in or close to the nick below the opposite side wall- so that ultimately the shot has an effect similar to that of an angle or cross- court drop. Playing a boast demands strict attention to stance: facing the back wall, with your body at a right-angle to the side wall and your left foot abut 2ft. from the side wall. Though it depends on how quickly you have been able to get into position, that left foot will be almost parallel with the side wall and pointing towards the back corner.

This is the only stance from which you have room to exploit a normal swing and the power it provides. So it is essential to turn your back on the front wall and get your body round and down- you must obviously get your racket under the ball it you are to hit upwards. There is nothing tricky about the swing itself-it is the stroke used for the ordinary drive, On impact the ball will be between the side wall and your left foot and between the side wall and your right foot on the side wall and your right foot on the backhand. Make sure that you get your foot beside the ball: to do this you will usually have to get to the back of the court in a hurry. So if you anticipate the need for a boast, move fast. As you will be in a corner, it is essential that, immediately after impact, you push back towards the middle of the court. A swift recovery may be difficult but it is necessary. After all, a boast travels on a long journey and takes some time to reach its destination. Your opponent is hardly likely to be caught napping. He can anticipate where your boast is heading and, even if it arrives bang on target, he should get there in ample time to play his next shot. So unless, having boasted, you nip back to the middle of the court like lightning, he will have you at his mercy.

We may as well face the fact that at almost every level of the game the ultimate destination of a boast often depends as much on luck as it does on technique. The boast is, in fact, a calculated risk. But frequently it is the only stroke you can attempt, because nothing else is "on". It may go down, or offer your opponent an easy kill. But it should enable you to keep the rally going and draw your opponent to the front of the court while you hustle up to the middle of the court, ready to seize the slightest chance of regaining the initiative. When luck a good boast may even turn out to be a winning "nick". One way and another, it can be a firm friend in time of trouble, and happily it is easy to practise: go to a back corner, organize your stance, drop the ball, and bang away. Keep at it until you achieve control over the shot.

Double boast

This time the ball hits the nearest side wall and rebounds first onto the other side wall, than onto the front wall, before falling to its death. Geometric precision of this nature is deliberately attempted only by absent-minded megalomaniac.. The sort who, in football, try to score goals from the hallway line. So the double boast is seldom, if ever, played on purpose. It happens by accident.

Back-wall boast

You cannot get more defensive than this. There is even a school of thought who consider that the shot should be banned altogether, since it is an admission of defeat. This is nonsense. The shot is perfectly legal and on rare occasions may keep a rally going when there is nothing else to try- when not even a single boast is possible. The back-wall boast means that you have been convicted and sentenced, but are appealing for a reprieve in the hope of a pardon. It remains the black sheep of the boast family. It is not really a boast at all: rather a lob in reverse. The back-wall boast occurs only when the ball has beaten you to the back of the court. But as you hare after the ball you notice that for a second- either just before the ball reaches the back wall, or just after rebounding from it-- you can get in a shot. So you hit the ball upwards onto the back wall in the hope that it will carry to the front wall before bouncing. This is the only shot in squash which is played when the ball is between the striker and the back wall. As we say, it is a lob in reverse, so there should be no- need for violence. On last point. Never regard the back-wall boast as a substitute for correct positioning . If there is the slightest chance of getting into position in time to play a constructive shot, do so. Don't hang about, ponderously idle, using the back-wall boast to save your legs and lungs. It is sloppy squash and will never do you much good.

14

DROP SHOT

A golfer can play a good round with only four clubs, because he knows which clubs are essential and which are not. In the same way squash can be reduced to four basic shot drive, drop shot, angle, and lob. You can play these strokes in various ways, and you can add others to your armoury: but you will get nowhere as a squash player until you have mastered " the big four". The drive and the angle we have already discussed. Now we can turn to the silent weapon that kills by strewth- the drop shot. This is played gently but firmly on to the front wall, just above the tin, towards either corner. It should be slightly angled so that, after rebounding from the front wall, it falls immediately to die in the nick, Even if the ball misses the nick, it should cling closely to the side wall and therefore be difficult to return. It is such a soft little shot that the ball should bounce twice before your opponent can reach its. Always play the drop shot to a corner, where it is more difficult to deal with and more effective in getting your opponent out of position,

A slow ball and a cold court provide the ideal conditions for a perfect drop shot. It will seldom be a winner on a hot court unless it is played with flawless control-or unless tiring opponent has first been drawn well out of position. But this question of first getting the opponent out of position, at the back of the court, is vital to successful use of the drop shot in any conditions. If you have made your opponent boast, a drop shot is the obvious way to press home your advantage. Just as obvious is the value of a drop shot when your opponent is tiring and can no longer get up the court quickly : a few drop shots will then use up the last dregs of his energy, and break his heart too. Never play a drop shot when your opponent is in front of you, unless he is hurrying backwards at such a rate that the sudden need to stop and go forwards may be beyond him. The drop in short, has two fundamental uses, both of them offensive: to get your opponent out of position, or to finish him off when he is already out of position.

The shot can be effectively disguised by adjustments in your wrist action. This will make it difficult for your opponent to anticipate which corner your drop shot is going to. He may even expect a lob, since your positioning, and the way you lean forward towards the ball, are much the same for both shots. In fact, as far as your opponent is concerned, not fewer than seven shots are "on" -a straight drop shot, a drop shot angled off the side wall, a cross court drop, a lob, an angle, a straight drive, or a cross court drive. So that when you move into position to play a drop shot, the other chap can never be sure what you are up to. Just one word of warning: before learning to mask your intentions by subtle wrist-work, concentrate on mastering the basic weapon, the drop shot towards the nearest front corner. Because this is the one we are talking about when we say the drop is amount the game's four essential strokes.

The front of the court is the best place for launching drop shots. We can be even more specific and outline an imaginary box from which these shots should be played. The back of the box is the short line. The front is parallel with the short line, but three yards nearer the

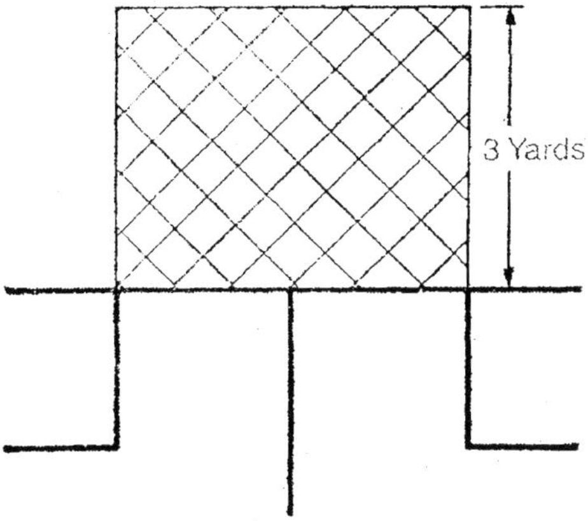

front wall. The sides of out box are imaginary continuations- towards the front wall- of the inner lines of the service boxes. This sounds complicated, but it is not: once on court, you can easily work out where the "drop shot box" is situated. And whenever the course of a rally brings you into that area, you will know that a drop shot is "on", as long as the other chap is out of position. Newcomers to the game should never attempt a drop shot from farther back than the service boxes, and seldom from even that far back. It is a difficult shot to play accurately from the back of the court, and the novice who ignores this warning will find "long" drops a costly investment. But if you are in good form, and the game is firmly in your control, try a long drop as an experiment. If it comes off, yours opponent will react like a started rabbit. But basically these long drops require a natural aptitude plus a perfect touch. They are best left alone until your game has thoroughly matured.

The drop shot should never be played in a hurry, because immaculate control is essential. So get into position quickly, and steady yourself before stroking the ball. Do not run directly towards the ball- run so that , as usual, you get the ball between you and the side wall before impact. Having arrived in the right place, adopt the stance you would adopt for a drive. You may use a full swing, to keep your opponent guessing until the last second. But the part of a swing that really counts on a drop shot is shorter than usual. That swing must be smooth, gentle, and carefully controlled. Hit through the usual line- parallel with an imaginary line from the toes of one foot to the toes of the other. Keep the face of the racket open, because this will apply spin and bring the ball down sharply after it has hit the front wall. The wrist and fingers are in command all the way. The ball is not so much hit as stroked. On impact with the racket, the ball should be level with the top of the tin, or perhaps slightly lower-never higher, which makes the drop shot more risky. Watch the ball closely, get down to the shot, and keep your body still as you play.

So far we have discussed the straight drop-that is, a drop played towards the nearest front corner. This is the basic drop, a vital component of your game. Practice is easy: start near the front wall get your touch right, and once you can play the shot accurately gradually move back until you are practising it from the vicinity of the short line. When you can use this shot effectively in match play, you can begin to develop one or two variations. The obvious one is the cross-court drop, played towards the most distant front corner, with the ball brushing the front wall on the way. In this case your stance brings you round to face the side wall, but at the moment of impact the ball is between you and the front wall. The angle of your approach to the ball normally dictates whether your drop shot is played straight or cross-court. Once you have the hang of both the straight and cross-court drops, you will learn to disguise your intentions by subtle little variations in stance and wrist-work. But master the simple things basic squash before you start messing about with the clever stuff, which in any case will be seldom used. Another crafty but terribly difficult variant is a topspin drop shot played as a half-volley. This requires such faultless timing that it happens more often by accident than design. Often you will play a drop shot on the volley. This is very risky if the ball is travelling fast, because the consummate control you need is almost impossible. Even when the ball is travelling at a moderate speed, the volleyed drop shot demands perfect positioning and stroke control.

One last important note. The straight drop shot often causes lets or collisions. This is because a man who has played a drop shot naturally wants to get back to the middle of the court by the shortest possible route, as he does after playing any shot. But in the case of a drop shot, that shortest possible route will find him backing away towards mid-court while the opponent is travelling on the same path in the opposite direction-in order to return the drop shot, which is hovering about in the front corner.

15

VOLLEY

The volley comes in many varieties, because during a rally the word covers all shots played before the ball touches the floor. So you can play an angled volley, a drop volley, and so on. The stroke is a volley because you hit the ball at a particular time; it becomes an angled or drop volley because you hit in a particular way. Most of your volleys will be played from the vicinity of the short line.

This usually means taking the ball early, when its pace is normally faster and the arc of its flight less predictable-than is the case after a bounce. Small wonder that volleys provide every match with the bulk of its mistakes. There are so many possibilities of error when volleying that you should not be too ambitious in your intentions. As a preliminary safety precaution, aim about 6 in. above the tin-no lower-if you re attempting a winner.

The vital thing is to keep your eye on the ball, to watch the ball right onto the racket. In addition, quick footwork is essential, whether you are moving forwards, backwards, or sideways. In short, make up your mind; get into position fast; steady yourself; and watch the ball, like a hawk. Don't make the mistake of looking at the place to which you intend to hit the ball. This spells error. Instead, look at the ball itself.

Now for the volley's uses. These can be roughly

grouped under three main headings- attacking, defensive, and tactical. In attack, the volley enables you to intercept a cross-court drive, thus suddenly increasing the pace of a rally and taking your opponent by surprise. The volley also helps you to maintain a fast pace against an opponent who prefers a slower game. If is out of position, a well-placed volley may even give you an outright winner. In defence, when you are caught out of position in the front of the court, or on the wrong foot, a volley can cut off a shot that is passing you and looks like finding a good length in one of the back corners- a shot that, once past you, would be difficult or even impossible to return.

The same thing applies when, farther back in the court, you have to return a service that looks like dropping on a perfect length. Another defensive use of the volley is, of course, on those odd occasions when you are scrambling about in the front of the court and suddenly find the ball coming straight at you off the front wall. Tactically, the volley's main uses are to help you to speed up the game, stay in mid-court, and cut down the amount of running you have to do.

But to play this sort of game consistently, you need to be a bit of an acrobat, with fast reflexes and a sure touch. The volley also has a less exciting but more essential tactical role: in returning service it is often the only stroke you can play; but, if well placed, it will help you to take over the mid-court position that is the hub of tactical supremacy.

When you play a volley deliberately, try to set yourself as you would for an ordinary drive-facing the side wall. Get into position quickly, than stand still, knees bent.... Your stillness is that of a tiger poised for the spring. Remember that as you get into position your racket must do the same- drawn back, in readiness for the stroke. Otherwise you will "snatch" at the ball and bungle the shot. At the start of the stroke your upper arm should be near the body. Your swing depends on the speed with which the ball is coming your way, and where you want to put it. But on the whole your swing will be shorter than usual. To get the control you need, it is important to keep the wrist low, with the head of the racket well above the wrist. Learn forward into the shot. Smack the ball when it is between you and the side wall. As you play the stroke, you weight moves from the back foot to the front foot.

When there is no apply pace and you want to play a gentle volley onto the front wall- the drop volley all you really require is a firm push at the ball. Cut the ball downwards so that it will die quickly after rebounding from the front wall. Experience will teach you to play the drop volley only off a slow-moving ball, and to apply both cut and slice to hasten the ball's death.

This bring us to the stop volley, which you need on those occasions when the ball is coming at you like a bullet carrying the twin dangers that you will be utterly beaten if the ball passes you, or perforated if it doesn't. It should go without saying that there is hardly any swing to this shot: for one thing, you have not time. All you can do is to try for a drop shot, keeping your wrist firm and letting the ball hit a "dead" racket. Obviously this is a difficult shot to play well. It demands fast reflexes and a sure touch.

Another form so the volley is the smash, similar to that in tennis. There is always a tendency to be violent when playing a high volley, but they are usually awkward shots to play, and in any case placing is more important than power. The ball, we repeat, must be watched right onto the racket. If you are lucky enough to find the ball coming your way at just the right height and speed for a full-blooded smash, remember this: you will not put the ball "away" unless your placing is sensible and accurate. The side-wall smash, is which you use the nearest side wall to defect the course of your shot, can be an effective surprise item.

But it is difficult to play accurately-and is squash, accuracy is more important than naked violence. It follows that to play a smash with any degree of safety, you need to be in the front of the court. To attempt a winning smash from the back of the court makes about as much sense as driving round a hairpin bend at 50 miles an hour.

16

HALF-VOLLEY

The basic, orthodox strokes are all played either before or after the ball has bounced. The half-volley is the tricky customer in the middle. It is a hybrid shot, springing from momentary inspiration or need. After all, you can hardly base your whole strategy on playing shots as the ball is just coming off the floor: if squash was slow enough and simple enough to permit that sort of thinking it would hardly be worth playing. So the half-volley is never planned more than a second in advance. It just happens..... when you and the ball get together in a handy proximity. By a "handy proximity" we mean the sort of situation that occurs in cricket when a batsman gets body and bat right to the pitch of the ball so that he can drive it, almost off his toes. To carry the cricket parallel a little further, it is important to keep your head down. Otherwise all you will feel of the ball is the draught it makes going by.

The half-volley is useful in both attack and defence. In attack it can be used to take the ball early and thus speed up the game, surprising your opponent and perhaps catching him out of position, with no time for a more orthodox stroke- you need to intercept a shot that would otherwise leave you stranded. It will then keep the rally going and give you time to recover to mid-court. In these circumstances it is obviously played in a hurry and demands perfect timing if it is to be constructive.

But let us assume that you are using the half-volley deliberately, as a means of attack. First you must move your feet to the ball. The half-volley is played closer to the floor, and closer to your feet, than any other shot. It follows that you have to get your head down so that you can watch the ball onto the racket: in squash, as in cricket and golf, the consequences are disastrous if your head is up instead of down when you try to make contact with the ball. As for the drive, face the side wall. The head of the racket is open. Your racket swings so low that it will probably touch the floor, so the hand governing the racket will also he low. But let us not be too frivolous. The wrist is supple, and in complete control of the shot. The weight, as usual, moves from the back foot to the front. Impact occurs as the ball leaves the floor- and at that split-second the ball should be being in line between your front foot and the side wall. If you fail to hit to ball at the bottom of the swing and level with your foot, the ball will fly up and probably offer your opponent an easy volley. Follow straight through, just as you would in cricket.

17

THE LOB

Like the drive, drop shot, and angle, the lob is one of the four strokes essential to your game. In its arc, direction, and speed it is rather like a lob service. Its purpose it to soar slowly over your opponent, travelling just fast enough to reach one of the back corners, where it falls sharply and dies. The lob is a firm prop to lean on when you are in trouble, and it has many tactical uses. First if you have been drawn hurriedly to the front of the court, you need time to recover to mid-court, because you cannot afford to leave your opponent with an open court while you are scrambling about in one of the front corners. The lob will give you the time you need because it keeps the ball in the air for a long while. Second, if you are playing a hustler who is better than you are when it comes to playing a fast game, the lob will deny him the speed he thrives on. Instead, repeated use of the lob will force him to play defensively. Third occasional use of the lob enables you to vary the pace and flight of the ball during a rally, thus upsetting your opponent's rhythm. Fourth, there are times when mind and body both need a breather- when your legs are tiring and a rally needs "rethinking" because it is getting out of your control. The lobs gives you the respite you need. Fifth, the lob is one way of forcing your opponent into a back corner while you take over the important midcourt position. Sixth, the lob can make your opponent run while you save energy.

From all this, you will gather that the lob earns its keep in many ways, though its basic value is defensive. Height and a good length are obviously essential if the lob is to elude your opponent's racket and die in a back corner. If you play the lob well, your opponent can attempt only one shot, a volley. If he cannot manage this his only hope is that he will have enough room to hit the ball after it has bounced in the back corner. Even if the lob does not quite clear your opponent's racket, the chances are that his volley will be played rather wildly, at full stretch- and while the ball is reaching him you will have a second or two in which to start off towards mid-court. But a rank bad lob that comes within easy reach of your opponent will, of course, be banged away so fast that you may be able to do nothing about it. So accuracy is vital- especially in giving the ball height early in its flight.

The best and safest lob is played cross-court, to brash the side wall before dying. You can also lob straight down the nearest side wall- but be wary of the obvious danger that, at the top of its flight, the ball may go out of court. The cross-court lob is safer because it avoids this danger: at the highest point of its arc, the cross-court lob will be over the middle of the court, far away from any of the out court lines. All you have to watch out for are the lights and any girders.

The lob can be played from anywhere, but is most effective from the front of the court. When played from the back it is rather obvious- though even then it can serve a useful purpose, not least in shifting your opponent from the mid-court position you want to take over from him. As we said in the chapter on the drop shot, your positioning and stance for a lob would permit six other shots. For example, your opponent may anticipate a drop shot and start moving forward: an unexpected lob forces him to change quickly into reverse gear. Because the shoulder of the racket arm falls more naturally into the correct position on your back-hand, the lob is often easier to play on this flank. Reach forward and get well down to the ball, because you have to get your racket under it. There is hardly any backswing: just a flick of the wrist. As with the reverse angle and cross-court drop shot, your shoulders will be parallel with the side wall. Stroke the ball upwards before it comes between your body and the side wall. Your face will be turned towards the nearest front corner. The ball is not so much hit as lifted. Swing so that the ball is already rising as it leaves the racket: it is important that the ball gains height early in its flight. It should strike well up the front wall and then, as it drops towards the back of the court, brush the side wall. If you stroke the ball too hard you will lift it out of court, or it will bounce well into court off the back wall. Your opponent will be grateful for either contingency. If you do not hit hard enough, or fail to gain that early height, then your opponent-again grateful, but unwilling to waste time. So the lob has to be carefully played to achieve the height and length that are vital. But it is such a useful shot, with such a wealth of tactical advantages, that you cannot do without it. So master it as quickly as you can.

18

THE SPIN

Squash is basically such a fast game that the deliberate application of spin is a risky business. The chances of error are increased because less of the racket face than usual is presented to the ball. So timing and touch must be faultless. It follows that the golden rules governing the use of spin are: not too often, and not too much. Now that you have been warned, we have to add that the possibilities of spin cannot be ignored if your technique is to have the rich variety it will eventually need. Obviously there is a good deal of scope for spinning the ball by varying the swing, the angle of the racket face, and the use of the wrist. Top spin is not used in squash except for a few half-volleys, so the only kinds of spin we need to discuss here are cut and slice.

Cut

Cut is a natural- as distinct from a deliberate- spin Because in squash, as you already know, most strokes are played with the head of the racket "open"- that is, with the head slanted so that the lower edge of the frame is nearer than the upper edge to the approaching ball. This inevitably applies a certain amount of the back spin known as cut, which tends to bring down the ball rather sharply after it has struck the front wall. The point of this is that the flight of the ball is checked, slightly but not completely, after the bounce. This in turn means that- assuming your shot has been well placed- your opponent will have to travel farther, faster in order to make his return. All this concerns the moderate amount of cut applied to most of the strokes you play. We now move on to the deliberate application of increased cut-which you have probably seen used in both lawn tennis and table tennis when a player has to return a particularly powerful shot. It is also, of course, used in lawn tennis when volleying a fierce shot from the opponent, in order to bring the ball down just over the net.

In squash, this extra degree of cut demands that the face of the racket should be slightly more open than usual on the backswing, so that, on impact, the face in travelling both forwards and downwards. Let the swing and the angle of the racket face do the work-don't "chop" downwards as you would in table tennis, because this would drag the ball into the tin. You can use cut when serving, lobbing, or driving, to make the ball "stop" on a length instead of rebounding. You can use it on volleys and drop shots, to make the ball die in the nick. Whenever you want to kill the ball in the front of the court, you should use cut. You will probably find it easier to apply on the forehand than the backhand unless you have an unusual wrist. You should never use it at all when playing a side wall shot, because the spin would bring the ball down into the tin.

As we have already said your timing and touch must be faultless if deliberate cut is to be applied successfully. It follows that novices should not experiment with cut in match play. It needs a lot of practice because at first there will be a tendency to "lose" your normal swing and drag the ball down into the - or to get too far under the ball and hit it up to the ceiling. Remember that by reducing the amount of racket face presented to the ball, you are tempering with the orthodox and therefore taking a risk. So practise thoroughly. When the deliberate application of cut finally becomes a reliable part of your technique, so that it can be used with discretion in match play, there are two things to bear in mind: first cut carries less risk when applied in the front half of the court; second, the amount of cut you apply must be varied, or it will lose much of its element of surprise

Slice

A right-hander, playing a forehand stroke, can put clockwise spin on the ball by varying his swing so that the racket, as it travels forward across his body is drawn in towards him. Slice cannot be applied when you have to stretch in order to reach the ball at all: because that forehand swing must start a little farther than usual from the right shoulder, curve in onto the normal path as it passes the body, and finish a little farther than usual from the left shoulder. The angle of the racket false has to be adjusted so that the face is turned towards the side wall on impact, dragging across the inside of the ball. Because of this unusual angle of the racket face, slice can only be applied with comfort and safety when the ball is below the level of the tin. This means in turn that the head of the racket has to be dropped almost as low as it is for the half-volley. The effect of all this is that the clockwise spin makes the ball shoot away to the right at the greater angle than usual. So it would obviously be pointless to use slice when you are near to the side wall. Apply it only from the middle of the court, where it is both safe and effective.

Here, as with cut, you are tempering perilously with the orthodox, so slice must be practised carefully before you use it in match play. Remember that the work is done by adjustments in the swing and the angle of the racket face. Beware of putting too much slice on the ball. The spin makes the ball come off the front wall quite quickly and at a wide angle.

It aims to make the ball die sooner, and farther away,

than your opponent expects. But too much slice will make his job easier, because the ball will rebound off the side wall and come back into court, where he can play it without anxiety. To sum up, both cut and slice are too useful to be neglected, but too difficult and dangerous to be used by novices in match play. You are playing with fire. It you must get your fingers burned, burn them in the privacy of your practice.

19

RETURN OF SERVICE

The most important thing is to get your "early warning system" organized. Primarily, this means watching the ball from the moment it leaves your opponent's hand. Many beginners make the mistake of watching the front wall instead- a mistake because this reduces the amount of time you have for reading the service and deciding what action to take. Besides watching the ball all the way, there are a few clues to help you to detect the type of service that is coming your way. If, for instance, your opponent stands at the front of the service box and drops his shoulder to serve, you can expect a lob: this will quickly be confirmed by the ball's sharp rise high onto the front wall. It a right-handed opponent serves backhand from the right-hand box, you can expect a service to a length, down the side wall and clinging to it. If he uses an overarm swing, he has violent intentions. This means you have to be mentally and physically alert, ready to move fast. But you will have a chance to seize the initiative, because as the ball cannons round the back of the court, rebounding well clear of the walls, there will be plenty of time for you to crack it as you pease... if you're sharp enough.

In addition to all this preliminary "reading", there are several questions you have to answer, quickly, once the service is on its way. Is the service bad enough to allow you a straight forward volley? If so, play that way. Is tne ball going to hit the side wall? If it is, can you play

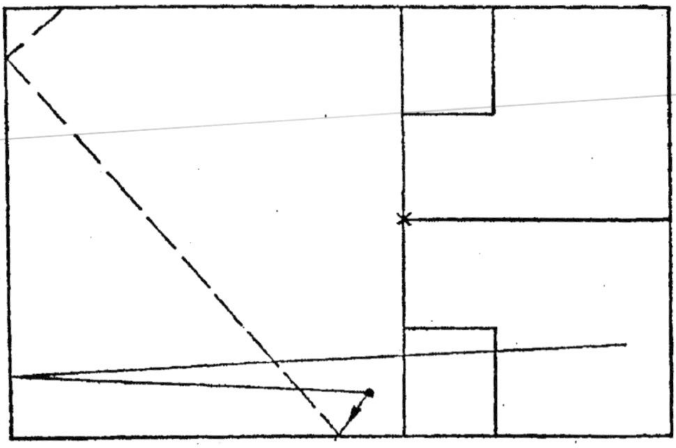

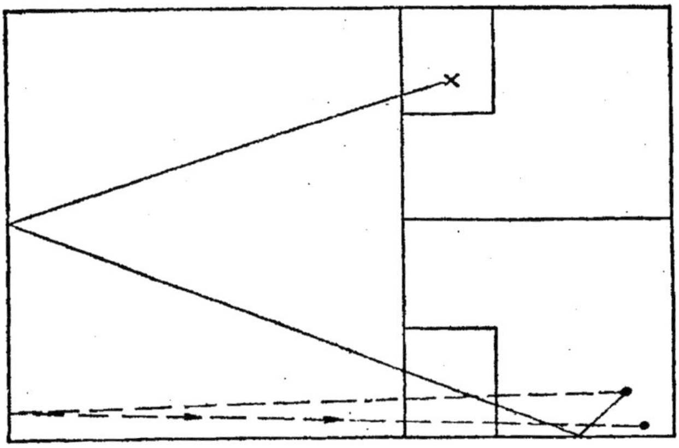

a volley before it does so? If you cannot volley before the ball hits the side wall, will the ball rebound far enough off the back wall to permit you a stroke? If not, volley the ball as it comes off the side wall. Never strike at the ball as it hits the side wall. Play it earlier or later. Make up your mind: don't dither. If the ball is going to rebound helpfully from the back wall, let it do so. Wait . Because this gives you more time to prepare for a boast or a driver.

Finally, is the ball going to come off the side wall at such a sharp angle that you will have to back away quickly in order to get a shot in?

Your position of readiness is obviously important, since you have to be prepared for anything. If your opponent has any idea of the game, he will put most of his services along that awkward line down the side wall, heading for the back corner. So turn your body towards the side wall. Stand about 4ft. to 5ft. from the half-court line and about a yard from the pace wall. If your opponent is making effective use of a lob service, you will learn to move quickly towards the oncoming ball so that you can go for an early volley. But don't move until your opponent has served, because if he spots you trying to " jump the gun" he will be crafty enough to vary his service accordingly. Once last point about your position of readiness: your racket should rest lightly in the fingers of your "spare" hand as your opponent prepares to serve. Immediately the ball is on its way, draw the racket partly back so that you swing smoothly into your stroke.

First, a good length down the nearest side wall. Second, a cross-court return high enough to elude your opponent's racket and hit the side wall, probably about 3ft. below the out of court line and above the short line. Third, a lob to a length, either cross- court or down the nearest side wall. Fourth, a reverse angle. This surprise item is hit hard and low cross-court, onto the opposite side wall, rebounding towards the front corner on your own side of the court. As the ball travels across the front of the server, momentarily pinning him back, he will have to wait a second or so before setting of in pursuit. Fifth, a drop volley to either of the front corners- it you are willing to accept the risk involved. This return is not a good investment unless your touch is really sure, because it is a difficult shot to play accurately from the back of the court. In any case, the ball moves so far, so slowly, that if your opponent is awake he will have ample time to chase the ball. But if he is not watching the ball closely, your drop volley may catch him unprepared and either beat him outright or drag him into an awkward position that will open up the court for your next shot.

No discussion of service returns would be adequate without some guidance on the puzzling and frequently frustrating business of back-wall angle-that is, the variety of angle that can be achieved by services rebounding from the side wall, the back wall, or both. These mostly enforce a boast, which we have already discussed in detail. Just remember that for every boast, the ball needs lifting, so keep the face of your racket open from the start of the stroke, and get it under the ball. As you move feet and body, get down to the stroke, drop your shoulder and wrist, tuck your stomach in, readiness, keeping its head above your wrist. Swing low, to get under the ball not only needs lifting for a boast: it also needs to be hit forwards.

20

MATCH PLAY

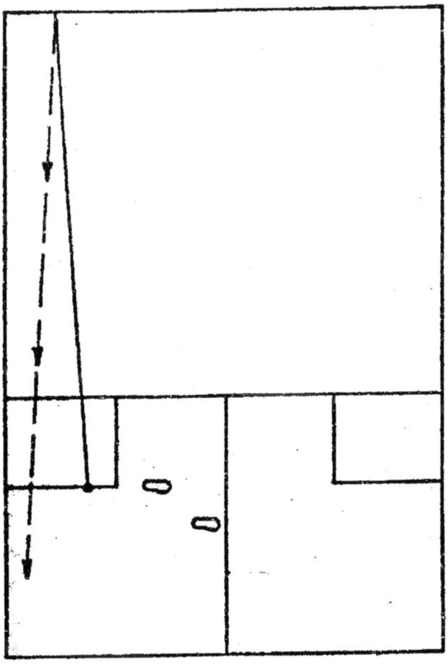

We cannot play a match for you. But in previous chapters we have done all we can to help you in a technical sense. Bow we move on to the fascinating field of strategy and tactics. The important thing is to be constructive, to think in positive terms, in order to get the fullest advantage from the equipment Nature has given you in the way of ability, physique, and sense. Make the most of what you have. All else being equal, a match will be won and lost in the mind. The roll of champions-not only in squash, but in many other sports, too- is packed with the names of players who were certainly not the most talented of their day. They won because they had the wit and the courage to push their talents to the uttermost limits-this should be your aim, too, irrespective of your basic ability.

Reconnaissance

There is a good deal that you can do before even hitting

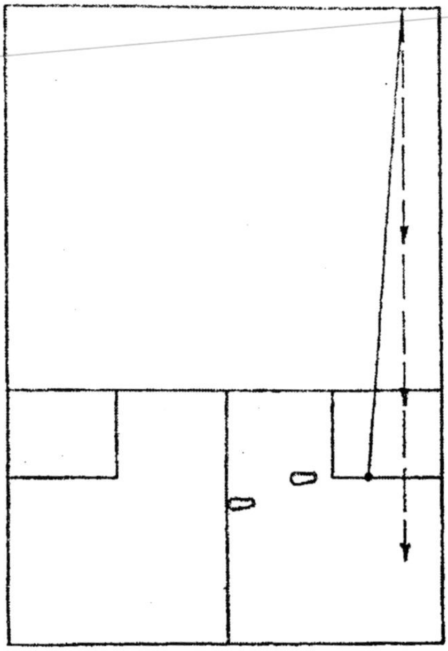

the ball. Later we will discuss ways of assessing your opponent from such evidence as his age, his physique, and what you know of his game. In addition, have a close look at the court and remember the notes we gave you in the chapter devoted to this. Note the height of the roof and the position of lights and girders, because all this will affect your use of the lob, Is it a warm or cold court? If it warm, the ball will be lively , the rallies long, and you may have to work patiently for your openings before going for winners. If it is cold, the ball will die quickly- and drop shots, angles, lobs, because the ball will just skid off the wall into trouble: all you can do is hit low and hard. You will learn to assess the speed of the ball, too. All these factors will help you to decide what sort of game to play, whether it will or will not be worth while to go for your winners.

One more point before you go into action: make sure that your shoelaces are securely tied, because if you have to interrupt the match in order to do them up, your rhythm and concentration will be broken.

The Knock-up

Never mind whether the order chap makes good use of his five minutes or not. See that you do. The knock-up is too often casual. It shouldn't be because you have a lot to do and not much time to do it in. This is your chance to get your eye in, to tune up body, footwork, and shots; to get your reflexes working, find your touch, and discover which of your shots are working well and which are not; to weigh up your opponent, and not least, to make sure that your opponent has his fair share of practice: there are two men knocking up, remember, so don't hog the ball.

This is the only time errors cost you nothing. So go for your shots and try to get them all working smoothly. Move your feet, too. Use the knock-up to require the habit of hitting your shots off the correct foot. Play backhands in the backhand court and forehands in the forehand court. This is another healthy habit, because if you play your shots in the wrong court during the match itself, you will have that much farther to travel in order to get back to midcourt.

Do all this you will be nicely loose up and ready to go. But do not ignore what your opponent is doing. Whether you know his game or not, the knock-up can give you an idea how his shots are working on that particular day. On the strength of all knock-up evidence, as to his game and your own, you can then decide your strategy for the first game.

Begin at the Beginning

The only time you can be sure of getting to midcourt first is when you are serving. Remember that at the beginning of each hand you can choose your service box, Do not keep serving first from the forehand box if you find that this is getting you nowhere- maybe your opponent is stronger on the backhand than the forehand. On maybe you serve better to the forehand court. Find out.

Central Station

The only place from which you can maintain tactical command is midcourt, poised near the "T" formed by the junction of the short line and the half-court line. Go on court alone and stand there: see how much of the court you can cover by taking one stride and extending your racket. Remarkable, isn't it? Not much can elude you unless it is in a corner, to high to reach, or travelling fast close to a side wall. And even when the ball is in these awkward places, midcourt is still the best position to start from in covering all the possibilities.

The lesson is plain enough. Move to midcourt, quickly, after every shot you play. Once in midcourt, keep your opponent away from it- which means keeping the ball away from it. If you are in midcourt, your opponent must obviously be in one of the four quarters of the court.

This gives you the straightforward tactical task of putting the ball in the diagonally opposite quarter, so that you can keep your opponent at full stretch. Never return the ball to midcourt. Put it in a corner, or close to the side walls. The point is that if you return the ball to midcourt you cannot go there yourself, because this would involve obstructing your opponent. And you must go to midcourt-so see that the ball does not.

Everything in its Place

Assuming that a rally in nicely balanced with each man in turn slipping in and out of the midcourt position, then the placing of your shots becomes more and more important. It is vital to get your man out of position if you are to make an opening for a winner. Let us remind you of some basic principles.

One is to put the ball in the part of the court farthest from your opponent. The stroke you use for the purpose depends on personal choice or the circumstances of the moment, since there is usually more than one way of putting the ball in a particular place. A second basic principle is this: if you see your opponent moving quickly, put the ball into the part of the court he's leaving.... he will have very little time to change from forward into reverse gear, or vice versa.

As with the direction of your shots, so with the shots themselves. Don't try to be too clever. For example, why risk that difficult shot, the reverse angle, when the much safer drop shot will put the ball more accurately into exactly the same place? We are not telling you to do the obvious all the time. We are telling you to do the obvious most of the time. It is difficult enough, and very effective if you can maintain your shot-control.

Make a firm mental note of the "accident zone"-the part of the court in which overambitious shots lead to a high proportion of errors. This zone extends, roughly, form I ft. to 6 ft. behind the short line. It is a zone 5ft. by 24 ft. which is a sort of no-men's land between attack and defence, a zone in which you should always be conscious of the danger of throwing your weight about without good cause.

Finally, in the way of keeping everything in its place, maintain a sense of perspective abut the scoring system. When in hand, you can afford to take a few chances and go for your winners, because even if you come unstuck, all you lose is the service. But when you are hand out, any mistake you make will cost you a point-so let your opponent take the risks, similarly, you can obviously afford to take more chances when you have a useful lead: but don't let it go to your head. As we said before, don't change a winning game.

Strength to Strength

Make the most of what you have, but do not assume that your "good" and "bad" shots are constant. One day your drop shots may be faultless. The next day you may be putting them down. This is something you can usually find out during the knock-up. Cut your coat according to your cloth. In squash, as in life as a whole, what was true yesterday is often false today.

If you discover that you have a particular shot that baffles your opponent, do not use it regularly unless you are in trouble. If you can stay ahead without that shot, why give your opponent the chance to get the hang of it? Save it: during a possible later crisis you will be glad to have such a weapon in reserve

How Goes the Enemy?

Have a look at the other chap. If he is tall, don't use the lobs unless you have to, because he will probably be good overhead. You may find, too that he has a long enough reach to intercept your drives. But he may have trouble bending, or turning quickly. Find out. If he is short, he may be quick about the court, but is probably vulnerable to the lob. If he is fat, he may give the ball a fair old clout but his stamina will be suspect and probably his speed too.

He will certainly not enjoy a lot of twisting and bending. He will certainly not enjoy a lot of twisting and bending. If he is old, he is probably experienced, so it will be a good idea to keep him away from the front of the court-where he could probably show you a thing or two. So pin him back and tire him out.

Now for his game. Find out his strengths and weaknesses. Starve his strong shots. Feed his weak ones. To put it another way, find out what he likes, and don't give it to him: find out what he doesn't like, and give it to him. Does he like a fast game or a slow one? Whatever game he plays well, disrupt it. If he likes the back of the court, driving to a length, use your short game to send him scuttling up to the front wall. If he is hot stuff with drop shots and angles, hold him back with drives and lobs, and avoid shots that will bring him forward- unless you are sure you have built up the ideal position for a winner. Hit hard, to knock his delicate little game for six. If a particular shot keeps letting his down, make him play it. If he is fit and fast, your drop shots may be ineffective and you may find that the only way to beat him is by deception by making him fitness, it does not follow that you cannot beat his brain.

21

RULES OF SQUASH

RULE 1: GAME

{1} The object of the game is to win by scoring points. Points are earned one at a time either by winning a rally or by being awarded. Each point won by or awarded to a player shall add one to his score. Each point taken away from a player shall subtract one form his score.

{2} The player who first scores fifteen points wins the game excepting that:

{a} At "thirteen all" the player who has first reached the score of thirteen must announce one of the following before the next serve

{i} Set to five points- making the game eighteen points.

{ii} Set to three points- making the game sixteen points

{iii} No set, in which event the game remains fifteen points.

{b} At " fourteen all" provided the score has not been "thirteen all," the player who has first reached the score of fourteen must announce one of the following before the next serve:

{i} Set to three points- making the game seventeen points

{ii} No Set in which event the game remains fifteen points.

RULE 2: MATCH

{1} The player who first wins three games wins the match, except that a player may be awarded the match at any time upon the retirement, default or disqualification of an opponent.

RULE 3: SERVICE

{1} The service begins the play of each points and is the striking of the ball with the racquet in accordance with this entire Rule 3. At the start of a match the choice to serve or receive shall be decided by the spin of a racquet. The server retains the serve until he loses a point, in which event he loses the serve.

{2} The server, from the beginning of the service motion until the ball has left the racquet from the service must stand with at least one and the same foot touching the floor wholly with in and not touching the line surrounding the service box and serve the ball onto the front wall above the service line and below the 16' line before it touches any other part of the court, so that on its rebound it first strikes the floor within, but not touching, the lines of the opposite service court, either before or after touching any other wall or walls within the court. This player must be in control of and holding on to the racquet at the moment of contact. A ball so served is a good service, otherwise it is a Fault.

{3} At the beginning of each game, and each time there is a new server, the ball shall be served by the winner of the previous point from whichever service box the server elects and thereafter alternately until the service is lost or until the end of the game. If the server from the incorrect box there shall be no penalty and the service shall count as if served from the correct box, except that if the receiver does not attempt to return the service he may demand that it be served from the other box, or if, before the receiver attempts to return the service, there is a Let, the service shall be made from the other box.

RULE 4: RETURN OF SERVICE AND SUBSEQUENT PLAY

{1} A return is deemed to be made at the instant the ball touches the racquet of the player making the return. This player must be is control be in control of and holding on to the racquet at the moment of contact. To make a good return of a service or of a subsequent return the ball must be struck on the volley or before it has touched the floor twice, and reach the front wall on the fly above the telltale and below the 16 line, and it may touch any wall or walls within the court before or after reaching the front walls. On any return the ball may be struck only once. It may not be "carried" or "double-hit."

{2} If the receiver fails to make a good return of a good service, the players shall alternate making returns until one player fails to make a good return. The player failing to make a good return loses the point.

{3} Until the ball has been touched or has hit the floor twice, it may be struck at any number of times.

RULE 5: RIGHT TO PLAY THE BALL

{1} Immediately after striking the ball a player must get out of an opponent's way and must:

{i} Give an opponent a fair view of the ball;

{ii} Give an opponent a fair opportunity to get to and strike at the ball in and from any position on the court elected by the opponent. A player will be deemed to have failed to give his opponent a fair opportunity to get and strike the ball when he has used an excessive follow through so that so his opponent has to wait for an excessive swing;

{iii} Allow an opponent to play the ball to any part of the front wall, either side wall or the back wall; and

{iv} Refrain from creating a visual or audible distraction.

RULE 6: LET

{1} A Let mandates the playing over of a point.

{2} On the replay of the point the server {a} is entitled to two serves even if a fault occurred in the original point. {b} must serve from the correct box even if he served from the incorrect box on the original point, and {c} provided he is a new server, may serve from a service box other than the one selected on the original point.

{3} In addition to the Lets described elsewhere, the following are lets if the player whose turn it is to strike the ball could otherwise have made a good return:

{a} When owing to the position of such player, his opponent is unable to avoid being touched by the ball.

{b} When such player refrains from striking at the ball because of a reasonable fear of injuring his opponent.

{c} When on such player before or during the act of striking or striking at the ball is touched by his opponent, his racquet or anything he wears or carries.

{d} When on the first bounce from the floor the ball hits on or above the six and one half foot line on the back wall; and

{4} A player may request a Let or a Let point. A request by a player for a Let shall automatically include a request for a Let point. Upon such request, the Referee shall allow a Let, Let point or No Let.

{5} No Let shall be allowed on any stroke a player makes unless he requests such before or during the act of striking or striking at the ball.

{6} The Referee shall not call or allow a Let as defined in this Rule unless such Let is requested by a player; Provided, however, the Referee may call a Let at any time {a} When there is interference with play caused by any factor beyond the control of the player, or {b} When he fears that a player is about to suffer severe physical injury,

RULE 7: BALL IN PLAY TOUCHING PLAYER

{1} If a ball in play, after hitting the front wall, but before being returned again, shall touch either player, or anything he wears or carries the player so touched loses the point, except as provided in Rule

{2} If a ball in play touched the player who last returned it or anything he wears or carries before in hits the front wall, the player so touched loses the point, except as provided in Rule

{3} If a ball in play, after being struck by a player on a return, hits the player's opponent or anything the opponent wears or carries before reaching the front wall:

{a} The player who made the return shall lose the point if the return would not have been good.

{b} The player who made the return shall win the point if the ball, except for such interference would have hit the front wall fairly; except that the point shall be a Let

{i} The ball would have touched some other wall before so hitting the front wall.

{ii} The ball hit some other wall before hitting the player's opponent or anything he wears or carries.

{iii} The player who made the return shall have turned following the ball around prior to playing the ball.

{4} If a player strikes at and misses the ball, he may

make further attempts to return it. If, after being missed, the ball touches his opponent or anything he wears or carries:

{a} If the player might otherwise have made a good return, the point shall be a Let.

{b} If the player could not have made a good return, he shall lose the point.

{5} If a player after striking at and missing the ball is successful in a further attempt but the ball, before reaching the front wall, touches his opponent or anything he wears or carries and under Rule the player would have won the point, the point shall nevertheless be a Let.

RULE 8: CONTINUITY OF PLAY

{1} Play shall be continuous from the first service of each game until the game is concluded, play shall never be suspended solely to allow a player to recover his strength or wind. The provisions of this Rule shall be strictly construed. If the Referee believes a player is violating this Rule during a game, the Referee may deduct on point from the offender's score for each violation or the Referee may default the offender.

{2} Between any two successive games play may be suspended by either player for a period not to exceed two minutes except that between the third and fourth games play may be suspended by either player for a period not to exceed five minutes. If a player is not on court ready to play at the expiration of the applicable time period, the Referee may deduct one point from the offender's score for each 30 seconds or fraction there of he is late or the Referee may default the offender.

{3} If play is suspended by the Referee because of an injury to one of the players, such player must resume play with in one hour from the point and game score existing at the time play was suspended or default the match, provided, however, if a player suffers cramps or pulled muscles, play may be suspended by the Referee once during a match for such player for period not to exceed five minutes after which time such player must resume play or default the match.

{4} In the event the Referee suspends play other than for injury to a player, play shall be resumed when the Referee determines the cause of such suspension of play has been eliminated, except that if such cause of delay cannot be rectified within one hour, the match shall be postponed to such time as the Tournament Committee determines. Any suspended match shall be resumed from the point score existing at the time the match was stopped.

RULE 9: ATTIRE AND EQUIPMENT

{1} A player's attire, including, but not restricted to, its colour, design, insignia, advertisements, statements and slogans, shall be within the normal standards of good taste associated with the game of squash racquets.

{2} A standard singles ball as specified in the court,

Racquet and ball specifications of this Association shall be used.

{3} A racquet as specified in the Court, Racquet and Ball specification of this Association shall be used.

RULE 10: CONDITION OF BALL

{1} No ball, before of during a match, may be heated, chilled or otherwise artificially treated except by the mutual consent of the players or by decision of the Referee.

{2} At any time, when not in the actual play of a point, another ball may substituted by the mutual consent of the players or by decision of the Referee.

{3} A ball be determined broken when it has a crack which extends through both its inner and outer surfaces. The ball may be squeezed only enough to determine the extent of the crack. A broken ball shall be replaced and the preceding point shall be a Let.

RULE 11: COURT

{i} The singles court shall be as specified in the Court, Racquet and Ball specification of this Association.

{ii} No equipment of any sort shall be permitted to remain in the court during a match other than ball used in play, the racquets being used by the players, and the clothes worn by them. All other equipment must be left outside the court. A player who requires a towel or cloth shall keep same in a pocket or in his waistband.

RULE 12: REFEREE

{i} A Referee shall control the game. This control shall be exercised from the time scheduled for the match and/ or from the time that at least one player is on the court. The Referee may limit the time of the warm-up period to five minutes. Or shall terminate a longer warm-up period so that the match commences at the scheduled time.

{iii} Two judges may be appointed to act on any appeal by a player to a decision of the Referee. When such judges are acting in a match, a player may appeal any decision of the Referee through the Referee to the judges.

{iv} A player may not request the removal or replacement of the Referee of a judge during a match. Any such request must be made by the player before or immediately upon entering the court.

{v} A player shall not state his reason for his request under Rule for a Let or Let point or for his appeal from any decision of the Referee except if the Referee permits the player to state his reasons.

22

HISTORICAL RECORDS OF SQUASH

First national association to be formed was the United States SRA in 1907 and the Association also held the first national championship in the same year.

The first attempt to standardise squash racket dimensions was by the Tennis and Rackets Association in 1925.

The rules of squash were first standardised by the Tennis and Rackets Association in 1924.

The first recorded instance of court building specially for squash was in 1864 at Harrow when four squash courts were built.

The first attempt to standardise or approve an official squash ball for the international was by the Tennis and Rackets Association in 1923.

The first country conforming to the rules of international game to form a national association and inaugurate a national championship was South Africa in 1910.

The first radio commentary on a major squash championship was at the British Open on 7 April 1951. Max Robertson gave the commentary for the BBC Home Service from the Landsdowne Club where the semi-final match was taking place between M.A. Karim and R.B.R. Wilson. Karim won 9-2, 8-10, 10-9, 9-5, and the second and third games were broadcast.

The first use of a four-wall transparent court for a major championship was the Transwall plexiglass court manufactured by Andren and Son, Stockholdm. It was installed for the German Masters in Cologne in October 1981.

The first glass backwall to be installed was at the Abbeydale Club, Sheffield, England in October 1971 by Ellis Pearson Ltd.

The first recorded televising of squash was at the Australian Men's Championship at Perth in 1962. This was achieved by removing the back door of the court and televising through the open doorway.

The longest recorded championship match was one of 2 hours 46 minutes when Jahangir Khan beat Gamal Awad 9-10, 9-5, 9-7, 9-2, the first game lasting a record 1 hour 11 minutes, in the final of the Chichester Festival, England, on 30 March 1983.

The first use of a portable court for a major championship was in September 1978 in Kings Hall, Stockholm, Sweden on the occasion of the Swedish leg of the PIA World Series, Perstorp Ltd. erected a prefabricated court with a glass backwall in the arena. Approximately 600 people watched the final.

The first attempt to standardise the size of international squash court was by the Tennis and Rackets Association in 1909.

The most wins in the Amateur Championship is six by F. Amr Bey, later appointed Ambassador in London, who won in 1931-33 and 1935-37. Norman Francis Borrett of England won 5 times—1946-50.

Although rackets with a soft ball was played in 1817 at Harrow School, Harrow, Greater London, there was no recognised champion of any country until John A. Miskey of Philadelphia won the American Amateur Singles Championships in 1907.

The first time that two sisters contested a major international title—Joyce Cave and Nancy Cave of Great Britain—was in the final of the spring 1922 inaugural British Open.

The first time two brothers contested a major international title—Hashim Khan and Azam Khan of Pakistan—was in the final of the 1953/4 British Open.

The shortest recorded match was when Deanna Murray beat Christine Rees in only 9½ min in a Ladies Welsh title match at Rhos-on-Sea, Clwyd, on 21 October 1979.

The largest recorded audience for a squash match was for the final of the British Open at Wembley Conference Centre on 10 April 1984 when the crowd was 2603. The court used for the event was the ICI perspex with four transparent walls. The previous largest was 1800 for the final of the French Open in March, 1984 in Paris. The court used was the Pearson Twin-Vue with four glass walls.

The first recorded instance of a player losing a first class match without serving was when Ian Wright played for Kent against Hampshire in the Premier Division of the Inter-Country Championship on I November 1980 at Winchester Lawn Tennis and Squash Club. Wright lost 9-0, 9-0, 9-0 to Aubrey Waddy of Hampshire in 17 minutes. The match was played two days after Wright's 46th birthday and it was his first appearance for Kent.

The first players to be disqualified by a referee from a major international championship were Ali Aziz in the 1977 World Open in Australia—dismissed under the rule that play shall be continuous—and Hiddy Jahan of England dismissed from the Chichester Festival in 1983 for abuse and arguing with the referee.

In 1977 in the final of the ISRF World Amateur Individual Championship in Toronto, Canada, Maqsood Ahmed of Pakistan beat his brother, Mohammed Saleem to become the first Pakistani player to take the title.

The first woman was Heather McKay who beat Beverley Johnson in the final of 1968 British Open. Mrs. McKay won 9-0, 9-0, 9-0.

The first man to win a major international professional title without conceding a point was Jahangir Khan who beat

Maqsood Ahmed in the final of the 1982 ISPA Championship at the Abbeydale Club, Sheffield on 10 March. Jahangir won 9-0, 9-0, 9-0.

The Most International Appearances:

Women: Geraldine Barniville of Ireland who has won 71 caps. She first played for Ireland against England in 1973 and retired from international squash in October 1983 after playing for Ireland against Wales in the WISRF Team Championship in Perth, Australia.

Men: Christopher Wilson of Scotland. He retired from international squash after winning his 106th cap and playing for Scotland against England in Edinburgh in January 1984. He first played for his country in 1969.

The longest span of internationals was achieved by Sheila Macintosh, the 1960 British champion who played for England v. Wales in April 1949 and in December 1971—a span of 22 years 8 months. Among men, Lawrence John Verney was only marginally less, representing Wales on 3 February 1950 and on 17 February 1972.

The most team wins in the ISRF World Championships is four by Australia in 1967, 1969, 1971 and 1973.

The most individual wins in the ISRF World Championship is three by Geoff Hunt of Australia—1967, 1969, 1971.

The most team wins in the WISRF World Championships is two by Australia in 1981 and 1983.

The most appearances in the women's British Open finals is 16 by Heather McKay of Australia, in 1962-77 inclusive.

The most appearances in the men's British Open finals is 10 by Geoff Hunt of Australia in 1968-69, 1971, 1973,

1975-80.

The most individual wins in WISRF World Championships is two by Heather McKay in 1976 and 1979.

The youngest player to win the ISRF World Individual Championships is Jahangir Khan of Pakistan, aged 15 years 10 months in the 1979 championship in Melbourne, Australia. He beat Phil Kenyon of Great Britain in the final. The 1979 event was the last for amateurs only.

The woman most times runner-up in the British Open is Nancy Cave—6 times in 1922, 1922, 1924, 1925, 1926 and 1931.

The youngest player to win the women's British Open is Susan Noel aged 19 years and 7 months in January 1932. She beat Joyce Cave 9-5, 9-7, 9-1. Joyce Cave was 19 years and 8 months when she won the first Open in 1922.

The youngest player to win the men's British Open is Jahangir Khan of Pakistan, aged 18 years 119 days, in April 1982 when the event was held at the Churchill Theatre, Bromley, Kent. He beat Hiddy Jahan, then of Pakistan, now of England, in the final.

The first woman to win the British Open final without conceding a point was Heather McKay of Australia who beat Beverley Johnson 9-0, 9-0, 9-0 in the 1968 final.

The most wins in the British Open Championship is eight by Geoff Hunt of Australia in 1969, 1974 and 1976-81. Hashim Khan of. Pakistan won seven times and Jonah Barrington of Great Britain and Ireland won six times.

The largest prize money for the women's British Open is £11225 for the 1983/4 championship, sponsored by Davies and Tate.

The largest first prize for the men's British Open is £4000 won by Geoff Hunt of Australia competing in the 1981/2 championship sponsored by Audi, and Jahangir Khan competing in the 1983/4 championship sponsored by Davies and Tate.

The largest prize money for the men's British Open is £25000 for the 1981/2 and 1983/4 events sponsored by Audi and Davies and Tate, respectively.

The largest first prize for the women's British Open is £2000 won by Sue Devoy competing in the 1983/4 championship, sponsored by Davies and Tate.

The most wins in the British Open Vintage Championship is by Hashim Khan who won it six times between 1978 and 1983.

Jahangir Khan of Pakistan has won three, in 1981, 1982 and 1983.

The most wins in the World Open Championship is four by Geoff Hunt of Australia in 1976, 1977, 1979 and 1980.

The most appearance in the women's World Open finals is 2 made by Rhonda Thorne and Vicki Cardwell, both of Australia, in 1981 and 1983.

The most appearances in the men's World Open finals is 5, made by Geoff Hunt of Australia in 1975, 1977, 1979, 1980 and 1981.

The youngest player to win the women's World Open is Rhonda Thorne of Australia, aged 23 when the event was held in 1981 in Toronto, Canada. She beat Vicki Hoffman in the final.

The youngest player to win the men's World Open is Jahangir Khan of Pakistan, aged 17 years 354 days, in November 1981, when the event was held in Toronto, Canada. He beat Geoff Hunt of Australia in the final.

The first woman to win a World Open title without losing

a game was Heather McKay in the 1976 championship when the first event was held in Brisbane.

The first man to win a World Open title without losing a game was Jahangir Khan in the 1983 championship held in Munich, West Germany. He played six matches, winning 18 games, conceding 39 points. In seven of the games he lost no points.

The largest first prize for the men's World Open is £6448 won by Jahangir Khan of Pakistan competing in the 1982 championship, sponsored by Canadian Club.

The largest first prize for the women's World Open is £1829, won by Vicki Cardwell of Australia competing in the 1983 championship held in Perth, Australia.

The first time two teenagers contested a World Open final was Tuesday 6 December 1983 in Munich, West Germany, Jahangir Khan of Pakistan, aged 19 years 11 months, met Chris Dittmar of Australia, aged 19 years and 10 months.

The first woman to hold both the World Open and British Open titles was Vicki Cardwell of Australia in 1983.

The first man to hold both the World Open and British Open titles was Geoff Hunt of Australia in 1977.

The woman most times runner-up is Sue Cogswell of England with a total of four. Three in the British Open and once in the World Open.

The man most times runner-up in the World and British Open finals is Qamar Zaman of Pakistan with a total of seven. Three in the World Open and four in the British Open.

The first woman to hold the British, Australian and American women's titles in the same session is Janet Shardlow of England in 1954/5.

The most team wins in the European Championships is nine by the England men's team.

In the women's competition England have won every year.

The largest recorded fine imposed is £1000 on Lisa Opie by the disciplinary committee of the English Women's Squash Rackets Association for bringing the game into disrepute while competing in the final of the 1983/4 British Open. Miss Opie was also banned from competing in the 1984/5 Open.

The most wins in the Women's Squash Rackets Association Championship is 16 by Heather McKay from 1961 to 1977.

The longest running sponsorship is by Banbury Grandstands Ltd., manufacturers of the Banbury Squash Courts. In the 1969/70 season they launched a national club team championship for men's teams of five players which was open to all clubs and affiliated to the English SRA. Prize money was £150 to the winning club and £50 to the runner-up. In 1976 a women's event was introduced.

At the end of the 1982/3 season the running of the tournament was taken over by the SRA and WSRA, although the event name was retained and the sponsoring company continued to make a sizeable contribution towards running costs. By the end of the 1983/4 season the Banbury Trophy had been running for 15 seasons and prize money was £350 to winning club and £175 to the runners-up.

Most Appearances in Major Finals

Men			
Championship	*Name of Player*	*Name of Country*	*Number of Appearances*
World Open 5, ISRF 3, British Open 10	Geoff Hunt	Australia	18
World Open 3, ISRF 2, British Open 4	Jahagnir Khan	Pakistan	9
World Open 3, ISRF 1,	Qamar Zaman	Pakistan	9
British Open 8	Hashim Khan	Pakistan	8

Women

Championship	*Name of Player*	*Name of Country*	*Number of Appearances*
WISRF 2, British Open 16	Heather McKay	Australia	18
British Open 12	Janet Shardlow	England	12
Brith Open 9	Nancy Cave	England	9
WISRF 2, British Open 5	Vicki Cardwell	Australia	7